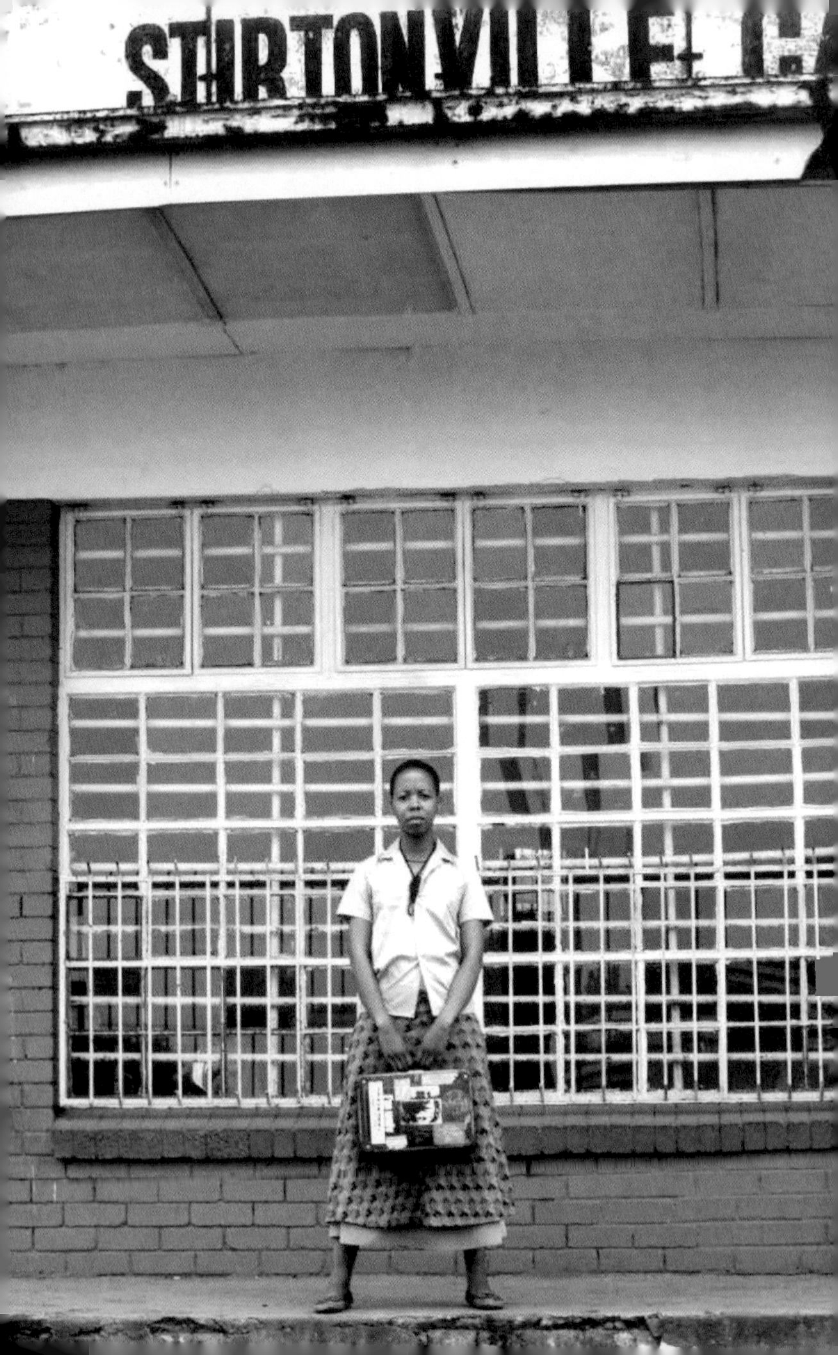
STIRTONVILLE

preface

Over the six years it has taken to amass the images and insights that make up this book, a common theme has constantly emerged and re-emerged. Everywhere we went, every study we undertook, and every client we worked with was being affected by a transition we are all experiencing, from an age of mass media to an age of "social" media.

My Western-centric view of the world, with its post-imperial prejudice and minority-world arrogance, was also shifted to a new worldview, one energized by extensive travel to and from Mongolia, Bhutan, China, Russia, Korea, Japan, Polynesia, Australia, Argentina, Antarctica, and beyond. I evolved a personal philosophy. As I met and engaged in conversation with people from all over our world, from many different traditions—themselves the product of many diverse and interwoven cultural conversations, economic experiences, and political contexts—I became eager to learn *from* people and places, not *about* them. "Learning from…" became the central focus of our work at the studio and led to the idea that we should collaborate rather than commission. Everything in this book is a consequence of those collaborations, with photographers, writers, and observers from within the cultures we have explored.

A long time ago I was briefly a high school geography teacher. I quickly realized that teaching geography having not traveled or worked beyond the place of my birth was ridiculous. I had worked on college projects with fellow students from Africa and the U.S.A. These other students challenged the orthodoxy of geographers who had observed the world from the U.K., the hub of a fading empire. A rambling road brought me into the international advertising and marketing industry. It was the perfect home for a person curious about perspective, narrative, and the long view. Since that time, my entire career seems to have been spent learning about people and places. I've always felt the call of new cultures. The incredible generosity of people's spirit and the enlightenment of new understanding have always affected me deeply. It's like constantly falling in love and then never falling out of love. I realized that learning *about* people and places was a distant, academic activity. In learning *from*, I was falling in, being "academic" only in the discipline of my strategic mind, but otherwise being wholly absorbed in my deeper consciousness—my own spirit, if you will. I wanted to learn from these experiences; I wanted to be changed by them, to be affected more than influenced. It was with this joy that we embarked on creating the studio, Studioriley, a place where we could explore the world for clients and help them think strategically, with a view to learning from people and places in this extraordinary kaleidoscopic world we have inherited from our forebears.

And the powerful change, from mass to social media, the one I had been a tiny part of instigating when at Apple; the change wrought by the confluence of mobile and social media technologies; the one that transformed the internet into the most powerful agent of social, political, economic, and cultural change in our history; the change that was seeping into every boardroom, challenging every government, and altering every conversation, from the farms of Africa to the online stores of America, from the forests of Papua New Guinea and the ice of Antarctica to the canyons of New York and the dreamy spires of Oxford, from the labyrinth of Tokyo to… everywhere, was accelerating.

To be in the vortex of such change, as we all are, is to know its chaos without fully understanding its meaning. From the view of recent history, there seems to be breakdown and collapse, the end of an order. But from the long view, the generational view, the changes seem more a transition from a period of history rather than the end of everything. We are witnessing the emergence of something new that is being informed by longer historic trends and powerful technological disruptions. This change demands some kind of framework that can help us think more clearly about what we are learning and why we feel so strongly that most of the assumptions we have been making ourselves, and are being made by our clients, are no longer grounded in social, cultural, or economic reality.

2017 is the fiftieth anniversary of Marshall McLuhan's seminal work *The Medium Is the Massage*. McLuhan was the first and most dramatic professor of media studies we've ever had. The book played with image and text. It reflected a television culture that was emerging as the most powerful medium in history. It posited that our evolution was to a connected state, the extension of our nervous system, and that our mass media was now our narrative, changing our reality. This clarity of understanding has only become more relevant today as our evolution continues down this path,

extending our consciousness into the internet,
a network of minds as well as computer nodes,
that is reshaping our sense of humanity, the way we
can work together, and how we coexist.

The November 2016 election in the U.S. signaled
a change, a delineation between two eras. It was
remarkable for the level of ignorance displayed by
mass media and the failure of social science tools—
the polling—to offer up a clearer and intimate picture
of the human condition in America. It was the last
time we could trust the mass media as a reliable
shared narrative. As the Mass-Age solidified, so
the power of creative insight had been sidelined by
metrics-driven analysis, forgetting that some of
the greatest insights our world has ever had came
from the minds of creative people, people who did
not have access to data. This illumination helped
us see the pattern that connected the dots as we
felt the change: economic instability, political
incoherence, aggressive cultural resurgence,
unreasonable loyalty, unreasonable disloyalty,
the speed with which new ideas replaced established
older ones, a breakdown in the codes of conduct
that managed markets—a seemingly endless list
of breakdowns. Creative destruction.

And from that destruction I felt a resurgence
of narratives that came from everywhere, multiple
competing narratives that offered adjacent
perspectives that demanded a more creative
reconciliation, a sense that powerful stories that
had been suppressed by the power of mass media
were now emergent and influential. The challenge
facing us today is not to simplify culture for
meaningless mass consumption but to elevate the
complexity of culture for meaningful human

advancement. We all benefit from everyone and we can learn from all people and all places.

With this book, I wanted to reflect on perspectives that grew out of our work, which has helped us lead a new conversation about our world and the role we, as business people, marketers, and communicators, play in that world. Between 2011 and 2017, we collaborated with photographers and photojournalists on more than forty-five shoots in locations around the world. We have created a visual essay representing just a small selection of this work. Each shoot was a part of our practice, learning from people and places, becoming part of the stories we explored. Professional photographers and photojournalists living in the places and among the people we wish to learn from provide perspective unavailable to the distant observer. The stories embedded are ours to understand, decode, and respond to. It is a visual language that can open us up to the world. Too many business reports are filled with too much faked imagery that adds nothing to the power of insightful narrative. There is not a single stock photo here and no Flickr theft. The photographers gave us the gift of their work, they answered questions visually, they confronted our prejudice and opened up their communities. It has been a remarkable, fulfilling, and exciting collaborative journey.

We also needed to take a few ideas and explore them in a way that would open up a conversation rather than close it down. This work is not a definitive work; it is an exploratory work. It attempts to start a conversation about how we can respond to a world after the Mass-Age. The themes that emerged from our discussions with clients and collaborators were the loss of trust, power of ethics, the transformation of culture, and the erosion of leadership. Each illustrates a challenge we face as we move from the post-colonial Western hegemonic enterprise of the Mass-Age to a new world of unregulated digital and internet media, the emergence of a far more rich and diverse interlacing of cultures, and new challenges to leaders of organizations.

Above all, this book is intended to be a thought-starter. A bookend to *The Medium Is the Massage*, but presented as a way to start conversations rather than define them. My hope is that the modest thoughts presented on these pages, and the idea that we are now creating our world after the Mass-Age, provides a context for creating a deeper and better world. At the same time, I feel a sense of incredible anticipation as my world, your world, our world, opens up and invites us into new conversations that enable powerful collaborations defined by mutual respect and engagement.

In November 2011, I was able to visit the Antarctic and follow in the footsteps of Sir Ernest Shackleton. The Antarctic was for me a place of powerful and dangerous beauty. We use the word "awe" too often to describe the non-mundane, but awe in the Antarctic is a visceral and spiritual feeling. It helped me feel my place in the enormity of time and space. I also immersed myself in the Shackleton story thanks to a wonderful storyteller named Mr. Kim Heacox, who was on the trip. As I sank into his storytelling, Kim helped me see something I had never truly wanted to see: my Englishness. That is, the nautical English culture, the lure of adventure, the stoicism, the capacity to survive against the incredible power of inclement elements. I realized that part of me, no matter how I denied it, was a conversation about being English.

My English conversation emerged again when in Dhaka, Bangladesh, with my friend and mentor Dr. Shahidul Alam, I sank into the decayed Victoriana of Dhaka architecture and listened to Shahidul's perfect English phrasing. It was evidence of the part of my cultural conversation that was imperial, the other side of that adventurous Shackleton sort that had subjugated and enslaved millions. And then, in the mist, surrounded by prayer flags flapping atop a Bhutanese mountain pass, by a white stupa, with my friend and National Geographic Explorer, Chris Rainier, as he photographed ancient masks and moved gently into the local world, I experienced with him the realization of how old and wise Buddhist culture really is. The generosity of the flags themselves, sending good wishes over the mountains to afar, to people that would never be known, in contexts they would never understand. With Chris, I discovered the power of unknowing, of embracing the transition between where you are and where you may be going.

The Mass-Age was a marvel. It was magical. It put men on the moon and placed control of fertility into the hands of women. It imagined a world unified by common values, hopes, and aspirations. It was powerful and it defined several generations. But it was also hegemonic, and suppressed values, cultures, and experiences from which there is still much to be learned. The collaborations now made possible at the end of the Mass-Age offer us the opportunity to grow in ways as yet unimagined, a combination of the old and the new knowledge.

To access this new opportunity, we need to stop the conversations that hold us back. In the West,

these conversations include the ones that justified
our self-aggrandizement with a romanticization of
our reason, our faith in logic and analytic thinking,
and the justification of our imperial power. They
are also the conversations that have marginalized
the creative in all of us, the artist and the outsider
voice, for it is in these activities—our songs, our
films, our poems and prayers—that we find meaning.
In recombining our reason with our imagination,
and sharing the vibe that makes collaboration so
energizing, we will open up the opportunities before
us. But if we stay shackled to our command-and-
control ways, our military thinking, and what John
Ralston Saul described as "the dictatorship of reason,"
we will be stuck. And it will be others, those liberated
from reason, who will choose to collaborate across
cultures in the pursuit of the unknown, who will thrive
in our new world, as it forms around new modes of
thought and new ways of being. ▲

introduction: fragmentation after the mass-age

The late 1960s were a cultural watershed. In 1969, Americans put a man on the moon and announced a "giant leap for mankind." Britain and France launched supersonic flight on the Concorde, a joint project that was to cement "entente cordiale." Just two years earlier, The Beatles sang to humanity with the first live global satellite telecast, "Our World," featuring the simple philosophical pronouncement that "All You Need Is Love." It was a song suffused with pancultural references, a musical globalism of chants, tablas, and guitars, and whose arrangements celebrated the harmonious coexistence of textures, identities, and cultures. The following year, in 1968, founder and publisher of the *Whole Earth Catalog*, Stewart Brand, helped distribute a now iconic NASA photograph of the world to its citizens, who had yet to glimpse an image of the whole Earth.

Technologies were bringing people together. At the heart of it was a vortex of mass media: print, radio, film, but mostly television. Jacques Cousteau. *Sesame Street. The Ed Sullivan Show.* Civil rights, women's lib, and Vietnam were broadcast in black-and-white, and then color. Love was all we needed—that, and maybe a television set.

Canadian theorist Marshall McLuhan had coined a term for this era: the Mass-Age. In his 1964 book *Understanding Media: The Extensions of Man* and its playfully named follow-up, 1967's *The Medium Is the Massage: An Inventory of Effects*—created in tandem with graphic designer Quentin Fiore—McLuhan questioned the fledgling realms of advertising and artifice. The Mass-Age was an era of mass media, mass manufacturing, mass movements, mass observation, and mass marketing. McLuhan inducted us into its values, its commercialism, and its tensions. It was to define the experience, aspirations, and ultimately the conflicts of the next fifty years. It would globalize the power of narrative, as commercial brands would sweep the world on the back of television's storytelling power and a world anxious to develop economically and move beyond the conflicts of the first half of the century.

From Procter & Gamble to *The Mary Tyler Moore Show*, *Star Trek* to Camelot (both the Lerner & Loewe musical and the John and Jackie Kennedy mythology), even the nightly news, we watched various degrees of fiction. Beneath the glossy veneer of these narratives were grand conflicts: capitalism versus communism, black people versus white, religious thought versus secular, women versus men, imperialism versus independence. It was the West versus the Rest, even Coke versus Pepsi. But for all our viewing, we couldn't see things very clearly. In the new Mass-Age, conflicts and cultures were suppressed. The brand was the thing, was *everything*. "American Exceptionalism," with its cultural capacity to absorb difference and transcend millennia of conflict, sold every Marlboro Man, every Stouffer's dinner, every Maytag appliance, every Cadillac, every pair of Levi's, every Nike shoe, and every politician. The Mass-Age was a tightly constructed and coalesced narrative, grounded in a belief that "we are the world" and that, under the banner of economic liberalism, globalism, and American cultural leadership, *the world would be a better place.*

The mass media both dictated and reflected our wants and needs. It framed our thinking and offered narrative constructs for all our experiences so that the individual was in or out, up or down, popular or not. What had been complex narratives of social evolution, of gender, of economic status, became simplified into a mass narrative. In his 1980 *New Yorker* piece, "Within the Context of No-Context," regular contributor George W.S. Trow argued convincingly that Americans were beginning to live in a world where there was only the individual or the mass. There was no local. There was no communal. The middle was being ripped out. Take the Nielsen television ratings: You either counted or you didn't— quite literally. This presented an impossible crisis for people: If you were just an individual and the only place in which you could find yourself was the mass, you would forever be lonely, because the mass would never reflect back an adequate validation of your identity and self-worth. You would either be absorbed or rejected. Either way, the individual got consumed.

The narrative was powerful. In an age of polarities, politics became about the mass or the minority. There was no room for complexity. In marketing, brands defined our cultural identities at the expense of our roots, our interests, our quirks, our beliefs, the values we share with only a few, and our relationships with the wider world. Blaring headlines and copy lines sold us stories like "I Want My MTV," "Mission Accomplished," and "Just Do It." The multiplex screened only the biggest titles and only at the most profitable times. At our fingertips, we had a finite number of radio stations, by which we could listen to a few dozen programmed, corporate-approved songs, or we could watch on television a handful of network channels and their sponsor-sanctioned programming. We shopped in sprawling malls and big-box stores. By the time Reagan came along, all we needed was "money"—a long way from the Beatles' "All you need is love."

Yet the underbelly of society kept peeking through the glossy veneer. We watched as corrupt televangelism stole the mantle of spiritualism, violence became a mainstay of entertainment, and the politics of division—a media construction of Red and Blue that worked the edges of America rather than the middle—created the fight that would boost the ratings. It was a media strategy that would spread across the world and bring with it the kind of suppression that, on the one hand, suppresses the conflicts the world is weary of, and on the other, fuels it.

Marshall McLuhan understood the Mass-Age early on, so much so that, with 1967's *The Medium Is the Massage*, he let a printing error stand. What was thought to be the correct title, *The Medium Is the Message*, as so many people now discuss it, became a notion much riffed upon by McLuhan himself. He posed that the medium, especially the non-verbal medium, was just as important, if not more so, than the content—the message. And his thesis grew more meta with each pun. The medium works us over much like a massage, McLuhan observed. The medium was, in fact, the Mass-Age. "Put the hyphen in," he said, "and you have the real message."

McLuhan's insights pervaded communications studies and media thinking throughout the Mass-Age, as defined by its primary tool: television. But the first cracks in this monolith appeared in the late '80s with the arrival of cable television, which was not tethered by the same regulations as broadcast television.

Everything began to change. Now you didn't win the ratings war by being objective; you won by being subjective, by segmenting the audience, not uniting them. It was called "demassification." The goal wasn't to get a majority of Americans to tune into Walter Cronkite; it was simply to get a particular subset to switch to CNN. It was, in media, what was happening in the economy, in manufacturing, in politics, and in globalism itself.

By the mid-'90s, the media was fragmenting even further, thanks to the dial-up modem and an uncharted virtual domain called the world wide web. Browser wars became the new ratings wars. ISP gateways battled for signups. But access was privileged, bandwidth was limited, and technology was glitchy. More significantly, content—and its creators—were nascent. Information, and thus identity, remained more or less streamlined. Culture was still something of a closed loop. The Mass-Age remained intact, barely. But a competitive human energy—the tension of subjective experiences, personal truths, and suppressed identities—still simmered beneath it. Suppression creates aggression mixed with aspiration. This is the root of the jihadist narrative. Suppressed people imagine a world in which the suppressor is overthrown and the once-suppressed revel in their freedom to be—and often their freedom to be dominant.

With the advent of consistent, infinitely networked media, the Mass-Age began to evaporate. The message was not as singular, because the medium was not as linear, as unified. To paraphrase McLuhan, *everything* started working us over. In the Mass-Age, one truth was dominant. In today's complex and interlaced network of narratives, truth is relative—and all truths have equal access to all. Whereas the power of communication—particularly visual, in McLuhan's argument—had defaulted to the mass in the Mass-Age, it now rippled throughout cultures, their tribes, and their members. A lack of diversity in message, in "truth," turned into a surplus. The once-hidden narratives of politics, business, and society became visible and newly active. This was when mass media became "social media," social being a more complex and flat network of relationships rather than a hierarchy managed by the economically powerful.

The mass narratives imploded, and the product of these narratives—mass culture—crumbled in turn. We began to toggle between facts and individual "truths," swipe right or left, block this or that person, curate our feeds or leave them "open" to algorithms. Whereas there was once a clear delineation between content and commercial, editorial and advert, the lines blurred. The broadcast media of the Mass-Age had the FCC. Our device screens have… filters? The mass market narrative started to feel quaint, and the Mass-Age culture declined with it. Every single sector is being undone, and consumers are running around having a blast because they can buy whatever they want, whenever they want to, wherever they are: goods, services, music, television and movies, games, literature. It's the stuff of culture, and the physical constraints are off. Meanwhile, everything that we considered in a creative industry to be a kind of trope—the brand, its consistency, its legacy—falls by the wayside. Post Mass-Age, we are bombarded with nothing but alternatives. It is not so much a Side A or B, or even a mixtape, as it is a multimedia playlist. And what emerges are new complications, new and competing narratives.

Richard Dobbs, co-author of the 2015 book *No Ordinary Disruption: The Four Global Forces Breaking All the Trends*, discusses this phenomenon at length. For most of the post-World War II period, "emerging markets" were seen as sources of cheap labor servicing Western multinational businesses. As the number of middle-class consumers grew, these markets were also seen as opportunities, particularly for luxury goods.

Today we see a far bigger picture, a world within which Western consumers are in the minority and people in what were once discussed as "developing" or "third-world" nations are creators of brands and high-quality products. We must recognize the rise of what many people now term the "Majority World" as a force within the global economy. And while Dobbs focuses his discussion on markets and business, I think this shift applies to civilization at large. We have entered a new age—small "a"—one that, despite our present divides, is not nearly as polarized as it may appear. We are simply less heterogeneous, more pluralized, than ever before.

The past provides most of the context for our present mindsets, and that is problematic. It must not be just our past but *everyone's* past; Western thinking, especially in business, can be very limiting when your market is made up of people who continue to live the aftermath of imperialism.

The American Exceptionalism of the past Mass-Age has a different place in this new Majority World—when we cannot think of cultures and nations in terms of first, second, or third. When the greatest technological and economic growth is not ours to claim, and we must look outside our businesses and markets to find innovation. When we cannot avoid the fact that we are but a fraction of that "whole Earth" of the NASA photograph. When our narrative and our culture are not the biggest things going. When we must reconsider the edges of what an "open" society means. When our media is no longer mass but—by its literal, transformative designation—*social*. The medium is the platform, and the platform enables many different truths.

Culture is the mechanism by which we adhere into social groups. It is a favorite song, a soliloquy we know by heart, a movie we love. These commonalities connect us with others. The language of culture is visceral. It is what we respond to, what stirs our senses and emotions, what we use to communicate when other means fail.

The language of culture is art. Culture is our collective creative history, told and passed down and understood through art. Art is how we share the meaning of our cultures, and, as Brian Eno has observed, it makes "culture viable and successful"; hence it is the method by which societies "cohere." And as a language, as a platform, as a variety of media, it is inherently social. Culture, Eno continues, is a way of creating "social solidarity." *Social* is not science—it is art. The rhetorical power of the Declaration of Independence. Churchill's claim that "we shall fight [them] on the beaches." Armstrong's "one giant leap." Dylan's observation that "the times they are a-changin'." Lennon's prophetic observation, "All you need is love." These are our truths—and truth is more powerful than fact. Our art defines our cultures and builds our society.

Whenever media changes, we all change, because media is how and where we articulate ourselves in

40

the world. Therefore, to understand humanity after the Mass-Age, we must become more alert to more peoples' cultural lives and identities. It is worth revisiting McLuhan's focus on the non-verbal, visual communication, and that NASA image that altered the way humanity viewed its home. The photograph is no longer a memory in an album, a slide on a Kodak carousel. It is the chief way the world communicates now. Of course the written word is a vital tool, but the majority of people on the internet—the Majority World—do not all speak the same language. The photograph has become a universal language steeped in meaning and truth, shared and recognized and interpreted, instantaneously and intimately, on social media. It is sophisticated, complex, has layers of meaning, and many narratives. The image is not the glossed-up "quality" of a *National Geographic* special; it is the human-felt articulation of relationships, with self, with close friends and family, with community, with place, and with the beauty and horror of the world we inhabit. These images are now easy to make, easy to distribute, and easy to experience. They fracture the monologue of the Mass-Age, they illustrate our differences as much as our commonalities, and they show us that the world can be better—but that it will be fraught with hard work.

But perhaps most of all, it shows us the multitude of ways we think the world can be better. It shows us that our view of a better world is not always someone else's. It reveals that truths are so much more powerful than facts, that the truth we experience is in the narrative that forms us, not the science that informs us. The Mass-Age attempted to elevate the rational over the cultural, the facts over the stories, logic over inspiration, and analysis over love. It did so because

the unifying impulse was commercial, to make
markets work, act logically, and be easy to manipulate.
Humanity is not rational. Reason is not enough
when we want to be seen in the world, unsuppressed,
elevated and validated to be *someone*. This is not the
Mass-Age. This is *after* the Mass-Age.

In December 1969, Marshall McLuhan spoke with
John Lennon and Yoko Ono. Two and a half years
after that historic "Our World" satellite telecast, the
trio discussed culture and communication. The beauty
of John and Yoko was the beauty of cross-cultural
truth. They redefined beauty. They attempted to
draw our attention to love as a unifying force rather
than social science, economics, and consumerism.
Ono lamented the shortcomings of the verbal,
"language" level, to which McLuhan quipped, "You
think you [we as humans] can talk understanding
right out the window." To Ono, the key action was,
instead, "touch"—not necessarily a literal one, but an
emotional one, a feeling born out of stories—of truths,
not facts. To touch, to connect with, to understand
someone, we must be *involved*, to use McLuhan's
word. We must experience, move within and be moved
by, to know *meaning*. If we stay within the realm of
rational conversation, true meaning can disappear.
And culture is not rational. It is not statistical, it is
not predictable, it is not absolute.

But the Mass-Age tried to be so. Let us look
again to its dominant medium—television—and its
extremes: winners and losers, ups and downs, Red
and Blue, us and them. Television may have eventually
broadcast in color, but culturally, it was always
monochromatic. And it was a ratings medium—
numbers, demographics, quantified data—and because
it was commercial, expensive to produce and distribute.

It was, like so many aspects of the Mass-Age, steeped in mass analysis. Sociology was being computerized. Politics was an approval process, and marketing, the application of data. The Mass-Age placed increased dependence on a decreasingly effective process of learning about populations. Analysts and researchers developed strategies based on broad, assumptive generalizations like age, income, and formal education. These numbers yielded surface context but little in the way of deep learning or meaning. Human choice was reduced to formulas, equations, algorithms, and in turn, a fixed outcome. The more the technocrats used data to describe us, the less we understood. It was outside-in thinking.

Humans and our cultures—those entities subsumed by the Mass-Age—cannot be reduced to science. This assertion is supported by a November 1869 article in *Scientific American*, of all places and times, which says, "A heterogeneous mass of facts does not constitute a science, any more than a rude heap of stones and sand and lime may be called a temple." We are not surveys or demographics or generational labels. Fast forward to 2013, when John Horgan wrote, again in *Scientific American*, "Social scientists are especially dangerous when they insist— and convince others—that they have discovered absolute truths about humanity, truths that tell us what we are and even what we should be." After the Mass-Age, the power of social "science" is reduced; it simply articulates a different truth, competing with all the other truths.

In a 1968 speech at the University of Kansas, Robert Kennedy addressed the failings of another metric, the Gross Domestic Product. He saw the

Mass-Age and was alarmed. "[GDP] measures neither our wit nor our courage, neither our wisdom nor our learning, neither our compassion nor our devotion to our country," stated Kennedy. "It measures everything in short, except that which makes life worthwhile. And it can tell us everything about America except why we are proud that we are Americans. If this is true here at home, so it is true elsewhere in [the] world."

What we are is culture, not data—and culture is about art. It is, to again paraphrase Brian Eno, what is not necessarily frivolous but also is not necessary. It is what we want, not need. Art is a hairstyle, not a haircut. It is cuisine, not sustenance. It is fashion, not warmth. Art is the means through which we identify and cohere as communities. And that is the emotion, the meaning of which Yoko Ono spoke. Our capacity to touch and be touched, to engage, was muted in the Mass-Age—and we grew tone-deaf because of it.

As we enter this new life, this life after the Mass-Age, we are now open to the power of art, of language, of imagery, of poetics, of filmmaking, of the selfie, and of the song. Our understanding of the world can no longer simply be observational; it cannot be an Excel spreadsheet or an infographic. Those days are past. They created the illusion of one world, an illusion that satisfied only a small number of economically powerful people. There are seven billion of us with seven billion stories, multiple nested cultures and worlds.

But there is a pendulum in full swing here. If we think back to the Founding Fathers of the Constitution of the United States, as they argued around that table about checks and balances, distributed power, and government by the people for the people, they based this structure on the words of John Locke and

Thomas Hobbes. Philosophers. Orators. Writers of
documents about society and culture that we regard
as masterpieces. Authors. Artists. The Constitution
is based on the work of artists. The United States
of America is founded not on science but on art.
It is founded on a narrative that emerged from
Europe about the nature of existence and the social
contract—essentially, philosophy. So why should
we rely exclusively on science now? Science helps us
understand *things*, and art helps us understand *our
place* in the world. They are different, and we need
both. But, after the Mass-Age, we *must include* both,
coming together in a new reality.

I subscribe, to an extent, to American
Exceptionalism, in that America changes more
quickly than everybody else. Our horrors are worse
and our successes are greater and it all works faster.
We experienced a civil rights movement in this country
that, in a way, predicted the course of the planet in
recent decades. The entire world is now confronting
the challenge this country faced during the 1960s: how
people from different ethnic backgrounds can coexist,
given a colonial history of slavery. Our pattern is to
confront a huge problem, let it get quite bad, solve
it through a democratic process, and move forward.
And things improve every time America moves
forward. We have never experienced a period in our
young history where we've faced a problem only
to go into decline—including right now. Whenever
civilization goes through massive technological
shifts—which is, in effect, what is happening with
media—enormous disruptions occur. And here we are,
after the Mass-Age, in this interstitial period of chaos
and uncertainty, before things re-stabilize around
new norms. As for those new norms, we do not yet

know what they will be—but our cultural instinct is for progression, not regression.

What has gone before does not prepare us for what we are now experiencing. Every assumption born out of the Mass-Age is being challenged. The mass is not the truth; it is an aggregation of truths. It is diverse and holds massive and ancient conflicts. Diversity is difference and unity is rare. The journey from the middle of the last century into the middle of this one is extraordinary. Technology is moving humanity quickly, and as it does so, it is opening us to each other in new and creative ways. Discomfort is the experience of change and is to be embraced.

At the same time, we need to beware how technology invites us to think the world is rational, that algorithms are truthful, or that data explains humanity. Science helps us understand our world, but it does so to give our world meaning. Only we can do that work, through our culture and cultural exchange. It is too tempting to apply the data of science to the challenge of humanity. It is the application of the previous era's currency in a new era. Social science, when applied too broadly, fails us. Now we need social culture—the storytellers, the artists, our creative people—to help us make meaning. ▲

1: the decline of trust after the mass-age

In 1958, nearly three-quarters of Americans trusted their government. According to Pew Research, that figure is now twenty percent. Trust in institutions is effectively gone. There are no experts, and there is no authority when trust is so low. This level of trust has been in steady decline for decades. It is not only a factor of the unregulated and unvalidated nature of internet information, although that has accelerated the decline; it is a consequence of the rhetorical strategies of marketing and politics, as both grappled with narratives that appealed to mass audiences.

In trying to appeal to the broadest audiences, industry and politics turned to the social sciences— this time to focus-group the message and test the right language. The banal and superficial generalities that offend no one also breed a lack of trust. The spin doctors, as they became known, existed to hide truth, warp information, and serve their own agenda. Instead of inspiring, motivating, or provoking, marketing rhetoric became about being inoffensive, noncommittal, and manipulative.

Political discourse in the Mass-Age, fueled by focus groups and polling, ceased to connect in a meaningful way to the very population it was intending to serve. Marketing in the Mass-Age was an extension of the same. It is unsurprising that people lose trust in their institutions when these institutions have no trust in their own voice. When all conversation is mediated by consultants who use polling data and focus groups, there is no conversation at all. There is no learning on either side.

Furthermore, the objective of polling and focus groups is not to be effective in serving truth; the objective is to win against a competitor. In the Mass-Age, the rhetorical game was to win on a massive scale. For example, tipping the behavior of the entire voting public by even just a few percentage points yielded power. In the Mass-Age, there was only room for two voices, each in competition for the dominant position, the shelf space at Walmart, or the monopolistic platform.

The complexity of a society full of diversity, color, and multiple competing narratives was blended into a meaningless mass market of simple ideas and concepts designed by pollsters and market researchers to appeal to as many people as possible in their current situation, rather than to lead them to a new place. Self-interest, in this scenario, trumped leadership. Political correctness trumped authenticity, and mass appeal was confused with mass apathy.

So, now, only twenty percent of Americans trust their government, and brands are failing, retracting, and diminishing. The new voices come from small groups, enabled by the internet and fueled with the realization that mass ideas frequently do not serve the needs and values of people, but serve the needs and values of the mass institutions, both in politics and in global business.

Trust is about integrity, it is about reliability, and it is about competence. And it is all undermined by perceived self-orientation. The fundamental objective of the pollsters and market researchers has always been to serve the self-interest of their paymasters and themselves. They've always created the sense of reality that they themselves then perpetuate. Today, they exist in an alternate reality where humanity is data and a limited number of analytics or algorithms describe the world out there, beyond their computer screens and business-class airline seats.

Consider the unifying goal for the Space Race, as laid out in John F. Kennedy's 1962 speech at Rice University: "We choose to go to the moon," he told a crowd of 35,000 people. "Not because it is easy but because it is hard." Americans rallied around the vision of our national brand—our flag—on the lunar surface. The government, led by John F. Kennedy and fueled by the speech writing of Theodore Sorensen, not a focus group in sight, asked each American to spend just $26 a year on NASA. That would be about $200 a year today. The product was pride, self-belief, excitement, aspiration, human achievement, imperial ambition, a sense that the future was better than the past, and... "Earthrise," the now iconic photograph—a literal vision of ourselves as the inhabitants of a small planet, unified in the emptiness of space, a literal and metaphorical achievement we are still attempting to deal with. The U.S. was founded on such ambition, and this latest desire for conquest, the race to conquer space, was a logical progression of the American Dream. That we could beat our Cold War rivals, the U.S.S.R., and return our astronauts safely to Earth painted our mission in an even more just light. It was a grand narrative of the next frontier. It was a Mass-Age event, drawn in broad, Mass-Age strokes.

We have traditionally relied on this narrative skill to knit together a nation of 325 million people. But not all issues are agreeable to all people. The Mass-Age vision of the Apollo missions was defined by leaving our world and looking back from the heavens. In Sorensen, one of the greatest speech writers in history, JFK found a poet who could elevate shared destiny. There is not a coherent mass, a consensus, today. This is partly because pollsters lack the capacity to inspire, because they are out of touch with feelings, cultural values, and the conversations that shape societies, and partly because the media itself has disintegrated and become less potent in defining a truth for a mass. But what is certain is that the vocation of the focus group-driven communication strategist, and the legacy of Mass-Age communications, is a failed strategy.

When mass media began to break down with cable television and ultimately social media, individuals discovered an easy default: Find the narrative they preferred, one more resonant with who they actually were. Media that spoke to subsets of the mass became more popular than the mass media itself; according to Pew, more than two-thirds of American adults now get at least some of their news on social media sites. But social media and its influential technology have further diluted the public's trust in institutions, and in some regard it has accomplished this by representing conflicting interests more effectively than its mass counterpart. Mass institutions present only a veneer across a complex and competing set of narratives.

In the early 2000s, sales coach Charles Green developed a formula: the Trust Equation. Its methodology is simple: To earn trust, you must demonstrate three things of equal weight or significance. The first is credibility, or what I term "competence"—a product or person delivers on a promise. There is proficiency of goods or services. The second is reliability—so much so that a consumer buys the same brand, votes for the same politician, again and again. The product or public figure is consistent in their competence. The third is what Green calls "intimacy," which is to say that a product or person is authentic, sincere, and honest. Intimacy connotes a personal relationship. Intimacy implies integrity. There exists a genuine, principled connection and an attendant feeling of security in this relationship. After the Mass-Age, it is harder to hide a lack of integrity because it is harder to manifest intimacy.

So, by the logic of the Trust Equation, competence plus reliability plus intimacy (and its consequent integrity) equals trust. The utopian point of view is that, if you possess all three, people trust you. You provide something that delivers, consistently and with decency, and your audience has faith in you as a result. At the micro level, it's why patrons return to your coffee shop. At the macro level, it's why citizens vote you back for another term. But in Green's original equation—again, designed in and for the sales sector— and as I have evolved it here, these variables can be either reinforced or undermined by the customer's perception of the company's self-orientation. Stated mathematically, trust is competence, reliability, and integrity *divided* by self-orientation.

$$TRUST = \frac{COMPETENCE + RELIABILITY + INTEGRITY}{SELF\text{-}ORIENTATION}$$

Here, the intention—the "why"—is pivotal. I offer you something good, something competent. I offer you reliability. I offer you integrity. But if you believe the reason I do these things is to enrich myself, that my motivation is self-oriented, you are less likely to believe my messages of competence, reliability, and integrity. Self-orientation does not build trust; it undermines it. Self-orientation marks the difference between a transaction and a relationship. It is the difference between the "we" of Kennedy's Space Race and the "I" of Reagan-era individualism, which ultimately undermined public trust in our institutions, including our corporate ones.

According to the 2017 Edelman Trust Barometer, trust in CEOs is at a record low, just thirty-seven percent, and fell in all twenty-eight countries surveyed—among them the U.S., the U.K., and France—while trust in the media is at an all-time low in seventeen countries. Self-orientation undermines everything marketed to us as the American Dream. Rather than elevate the experience of the mass, self-interest erodes it.

What's more, it crosses borders and corrupts seemingly altruistic endeavors. Self-orientation is subjective. It is presented as virtuous that Silicon Valley executives aim to connect the poor to the internet; such an aim feels as though it has integrity. But let us look at the equation: Every part is affected by perceived self-orientation. What does the Silicon Valley executive actually want in bringing impoverished populations online? Say a Western tech company moves into a Majority World country like India. From the country's perspective, the self-orientation in this Trust Equation is that the company seeks to line its own pockets back in the West. The dark shadow of colonialism is, to the Indian population, what we would now call a Western capitalist aim. When we consider these markets around the world, even in the U.S. or Europe, that sense of integrity is voided by self-orientation, which in turn undermines any actual perceived integrity. Furthermore, asserting a Western narrative of "aid," offered by powerful people to powerless people, is not by any stretch of the imagination an intimate act. The powerless are only powerless within the narrative of the powerful. There is no trust because there is only perceived self-interest and a total lack of cultural intimacy.

Building trust after the Mass-Age offers new challenges for two reasons. First, the end of the Mass-Age is not simply the end of mass media; it is also the end of mass manufacturing. As discussed in *No Ordinary Disruption: The Four Global Forces Breaking All the Trends*, by Richard Dobbs, James Manyika, and Jonathan Woetzel, companies the globe over produce high-quality goods in low volumes for unprecedented value. And "the companies that will succeed in the race for these extraordinarily diverse emerging markets... will customize and price products to meet local tastes and needs and will build faster, lower-cost supply chains and innovative business models in order to be cost competitive and deliver price points across a broad spectrum." No longer does one manufacturer have the edge on competence or reliability.

What does this ubiquity change? The points of difference are fascinating. How does the consumer choose between a hundred competent and reliable brands or services or even politicians? The answer is intimate integrity and self-orientation. The consumer, surveying a global market of offerings otherwise comparable except for those two variables, reasons, "I have to trust one of you, so I'll go with the one I trust the most—the one that has integrity by my own judgment of it."

Creative professionals end up in the middle of this dilemma because they must write the story. It is therefore essential that they hold their own integrity paramount and offer their clients the same standards. When values are shared, this is not difficult. Good clients will win, because people will trust them. But building trust is harder now than it has ever been. Thus, when delivering the message, when crafting a piece of communication, the corrupting influence of self-orientation is ever present.

Along with the end of the economy of scale is the transformation of the medium of expression. The mode by which creative professionals engage the client and the consumer, and build trust between them, has changed. Today's creative professional does not operate in the pre-internet environment of twenty-five years ago, when crucial issues of integrity and trust and ethics were managed by government bodies, industry bodies, and other enforcing bodies. Much of the current messaging exists outside of that regulation. Consider that we can say, post, and share most anything online—unless we reside within the Great Firewall of China, with its combination of legislative actions and technologies enforced as part of the country's sovereignty. Consider also, and perhaps not-so-coincidentally, that Chinese citizens' trust in their government is ranked the highest in the world at seventy-six percent, twenty-nine points higher than U.S. citizens' trust in their government, according to the Edelman Barometer. Sixty-five percent of Chinese individuals trust the media, eighteen percent more than in the U.S. Maybe such trust emerges from clear and present regulation, the known, rather than the wild and messy world of our unregulated internet?

We—all citizens, including creative professionals— are not only learning the new communication skills for the post-Mass-Age, we are mopping up the mess the Mass-Age left. In this new world, social statistics are at best equivocal truths if not downright lies. Data may be bigger, but it is ridiculous to hold a conviction that our understanding of the world is a consequence of our measuring of it. Trust was eroded during the Mass-Age by the communication strategies of institutions. In the unregulated cultural warfare of the internet, trust comes from intimacy, the one rhetorical skill largely abandoned in the Mass-Age. As we move forward, we will be challenged to speak in authentic voices, inspire using powerful ideas and images, and transform through truth. These are not the skills of the polling data-driven communication strategist; they are the skills of creative people: the artists, the writers, the filmmakers. ⌃

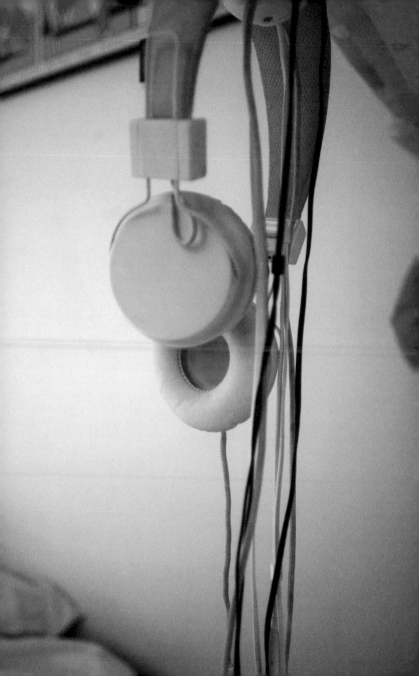

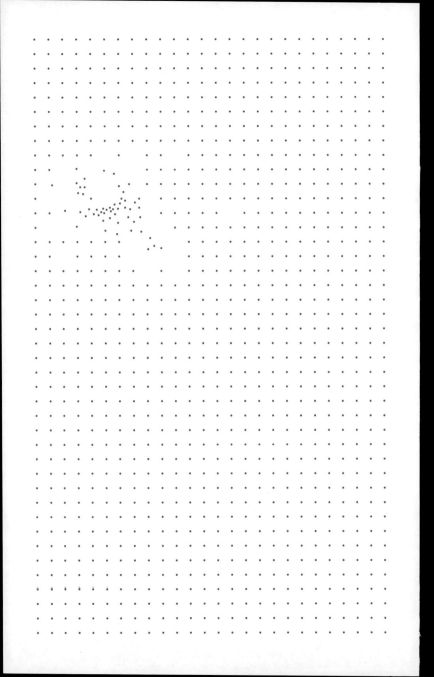

2: the power of ethics after the mass-age

During the Mass-Age, media was regulated. Broadcast television had restrictions on what could be shown, at what times, and in what ways. Commercials and sponsorships were regulated so the audience would know not only what they were watching or listening to, but who was paying for their attention. Ownership of media was regulated in an attempt to secure the democracy against the tyranny of ownership by a powerful minority. Around the world regulation reflected culture and political systems. In all cases, regulation reflected ethics, either agreed upon through a democratic process or imposed by an authoritarian government.

Regulation of media in democracies is always a bone of contention, but the general rule has been that unfettered freedom must be balanced by an understanding of the media's power to affect perceptions and influence the democratic process. Censorship is widely reviled in an open and free society, yet it is also—in certain places and at certain times—accepted. Pornography has no home on broadcast television and, as George Carlin famously satirized, certain words were not allowed to sully the living rooms of American families. Ownership of media organizations has been limited by law to protect the citizenry from powerful hegemonic forces that could limit access to the information needed to act freely within the democracy. The balancing act of regulation is a profoundly important role of governments and largely reflects the nature of governance itself, ranging from the constitutional democracy of the U.S. to the single-market rule of communist China. Media regulation is typically a formalization of agreed ethics, negotiated through the democratic (or other) process.

The end of the Mass-Age is indicated most clearly by the end of the dominance of mass media and the emergence of new—and unregulated—media technologies. The ethics that framed up the media conversations during the Mass-Age are largely absent from the new-media world and wholly absent from social media. There is a difference between, on the one hand, the implementation of socially agreed ethics upon a chosen media in a culture of free speech and, on the other, the adoption of filters and rules by a corporation managing a social media platform. Most business leaders would agree there should be policies—in effect, regulations—that limit behavior on social media platforms. But the same business leaders chaff at the idea of government regulation. Filters designed by corporations are not the same as regulations designed by governments.

This gives us a big challenge after the Mass-Age. Trust is in decline largely because the market for ideas has no rules. As most economists will tell you, an unregulated market is chaotic, and a certain amount of regulation stabilizes the market by enabling trust. The same is true in the market for ideas. Ethics are at the heart of trust, and trust is critical to both markets and society.

We have begun to see thoughtful implementation of ethics in the clothing industry with Everlane, for example, and its ethos of "radical transparency," an ethics-based approach to creating trust in its brand.

The product is direct-to-consumer; the supply chain is laid bare; manufacturing, (fair) labor costs, and profit margins are broken down clearly; and inventory surplus sales prices are negotiable. The entry point here is competence and reliability—solidly made apparel. The vulnerability and the power of a company like Everlane is in how, after the Mass-Age, it challenges the ethics of the sector. Does Everlane foreshadow a trend? Are they at the forefront of a culture in which we voluntarily adopt ethics to regulate the market for ideas in digital and social media?

We are on the horns of a dilemma, and perhaps a hierarchy of ethics, in that some issues affect people more than others. An organization may have an idea by which it can bring different levels of integrity or a different kind of ethics to an industry. The idea must be carefully crafted. If a company sets forth the position that a customer should buy its product because of ethics, this approach makes the company vulnerable—ethics are complicated. The organization can claim to be ethically good, and, in one particular sphere, it may very well be so. But someone may disagree with it elsewhere. Such is our challenge, to work at these issues.

One of the greatest ethical challenges of our times is to resolve the relationship between science and art. As science has enabled us to create new technologies of previously unimaginable power, our need for tools to help us relate to the world we are creating has grown more profound. This tension has informed governments as they have focused public education on science, technology, engineering, and math, otherwise known as STEM. Many technologists and designers, as well as artists and educators, have argued that such a focus is well meaning but underestimates the power of art to help us think, understand, and evolve meaning. The addition of the Arts creates STEAM.

Scientists and engineers are dedicated to solving problems, but they do so often in the context of moral dilemmas. Science-fiction writers, such as Bruce Sterling, William Gibson, and Neal Stephenson, are popular in Silicon Valley in part because they explore the moral dilemmas created by science. As we hasten ever deeper into a world mediated by technology—technology that has incredible power—we face the moral and ethical dilemmas such technology provokes. These challenges have left the domains of fiction and the arcane imaginings of scientists and have become part of our everyday lives, our societies. But businesses are not technology; they accept ethical responsibilities in discourse with governments and the people they serve. Ethics are an integral part of all business relationships. As we continue to feel the chaos of unregulated media, a consequence of all this advancing technology, we feel the need for agreed ethics. In the pursuit of trust, we need ethics—shared agreements about behavior—so that we can operate successfully in a relationship-based world, both in terms of commerce and in terms of society. Thus the job of the creative professional, much like the science-fiction writer, becomes to resolve moral dilemmas. And one of the ways to resolve moral dilemmas is through ethics.

There is a huge difference between morality and ethical behavior. Morality is personal; you and I could have moral attitudes that differ or even compete with each other. But ethics are agreed. They are consensual, a near-universal set of rules that we adopt for human actions. They are the basis of a shared social contract. They are the common ground on which we can have transformative conversations.

Thus, ethics must become central to the way we think about resolving the moral dilemmas our clients bring to us. And if we decide to opt out— if we decide that, instead, "My job is to be creative in the expression of my clients' desires, regardless of ethics, regardless of self-interest"—we will just end up with work that people don't trust. Creativity would become little more than a trick used to both deceive and divide. It must start with us, and with the goal of creating trust. The Trust Equation works to build an audience, to create trust with the public. But our efforts to make that equation work can often come down to ethics.

Graphic designer Paul Rand proposed the idea that we have a civic responsibility to our clients—that we actually do more than execute their will. In his seminal essay "The Politics of Design," Rand observed:

> *The smooth functioning of the design process may be thwarted in other ways, by the imperceptive executive, who in matters of design understands neither his proper role nor that of the designer; by the eager but cautious advertising man whose principal concern is pleasing his client; and by the insecure client who depends on informal office surveys and pseudo-scientific research to deal with questions that are unanswerable and answers that are questionable.*

Research and the social science practiced by marketing and advertising executives are permeated by questionable answers, quasi-scientific mumbo jumbo, and just plain untruths. It is hard to discern truth. Rand considers this a danger to design, since he ascribes to design civics and ethics. Ethics are not only the way we create harmonious societies; they are tools for learning.

For example, an ethic could be to never copy test or focus group a piece of writing. This would lead to some mistakes but far more successes. Included in this ethic is the idea that the failures inform the successes. Polling and copy testing have failed to create a cultural climate of trust. Focus-grouped messages have failed to advance human understanding, change minds, or even create attachment. After the Mass-Age, we can refute many of these approaches or at least limit them to specifically valuable activities such as the measurement of behavior. The behavioral economics movement does just that. These practitioners do not trust implied truth; they seek real truth by focusing on behavior. This is a huge shift away from research surveys by quasi-social scientists in the market research industry. We need to challenge the purveyors of polling and focus groups. They exist to perpetuate a language they control. A language that stifles pluralistic debate, misinforms on a massive scale, and disables good judgment.

In 1981, Paul Rand designed the now-iconic "Eye, Bee, M" poster for IBM. The poster was a response to a dilemma. He felt his client was losing touch with human reality. He was troubled by the dehumanization of business work, and he was concerned that the company was itself becoming more machine-like and less business-like. The dilemma has echoed down the generations and is found today in the tension between information and knowledge, a data point and human insight. The poster was incredibly popular in the company even though it remains an unofficial artwork. Ultimately a new CEO, Louis Gerstner, radically humanized the company, transforming it into a service organization in one of the most famous turnarounds in American business history.

For creative professionals to accomplish that which Rand accomplished, they must re-earn their place in the difficult conversation with clients about ethical and moral dilemmas. As the Mass-Age declined, the chorus of "creativity" seemed to rise. Creativity and innovation are linked in many people's minds. But the nature of the Mass-Age was not to elevate the moral dilemmas of consumerism but rather to hide them behind meaningless artifice. "Creativity" became "being cool" or "different" rather than becoming a meaningful part of a cultural conversation.

Attached to this imperative, though, is the need to step away and look at the bigger picture, and within the framework of globalization. We must depart from this Mass-Age axiom of "one nation under a groove," when instead the world is becoming an integrated network of economy and commerce. Threading together this post-Mass-Age humanity is a powerful diversity and, at the same time, the fundamental aspiration to do better for ourselves and our children. Underpinning it all is ethics. We cannot operate without consensus around ethics. Society does not work without this sort of regulation, self-organized or otherwise, and neither does the market. And in the Mass-Age, our ethics were defined on a mass scale. We were mass marketers.

But this ethical regulation, especially of media, has faded with the mass market. We cannot regulate the internet the way we regulated television. It is physically impossible. Thus it is up to creative professionals to regulate themselves, their work and media, and reach consensus with their fellow professionals and clients. I believe there is no future that is not regulated. I just don't think our society can withstand the hit. We have to develop new rules, an ethical blueprint for this interstitial period of history.

The work of Jonathan Haidt and the Moral Foundations Theory speaks to this mounting complexity. We muse on the world of today, one that is both increasingly global and increasingly fragmented around identity, and we are confronted with the fact that we are not just one. We may share experiences, emotions, and milestones, but we are more unique than ever before. Haidt's thesis is that individuals, communities, and cultures have recognizable common foundations—a handful of things we can all agree we truly care about—that form the basis of disparate views around the world. Fundamentally human ideas of suffering, hierarchy, and reciprocity are grounding concerns, the same across civilization. We share these ethical foundations on which we then create our moral structures—concepts of fairness, loyalty, authority, and liberty—on local levels. And this is the stuff of cultural and ultimately global complexity. Our perspectives may diverge, but, by understanding the nuances of morality and ethics, we can better understand each other and how to build a relationship of trust.

Globally, we are experiencing a period of instability, frightening conflict, the degradation of trust, and the breakdown of social contracts. Unless the creative industries—and the professionals who daily project words, images, concepts, and ideas into the world—come to terms with the power of and the need for ethics, this current period will be extended. For some, this provides the opportunity for authoritarianism and power. For most, it will mean misery. And for business, it will be a significant barrier to growth and success. After the Mass-Age, we need new ethics to enable powerful and difficult conversations to be had, with the goal of trust, understanding, and the elevation of all to a place of respect. ∧

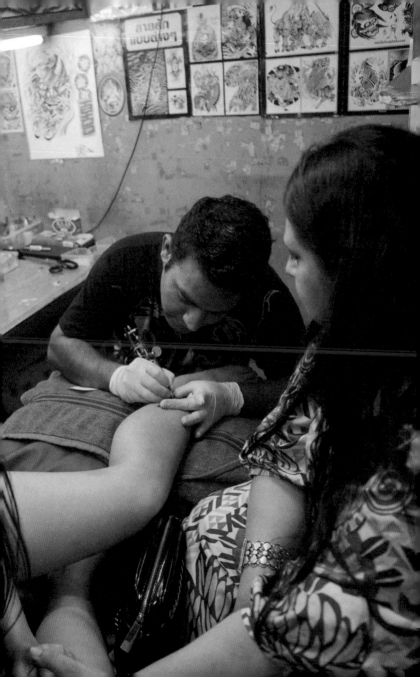

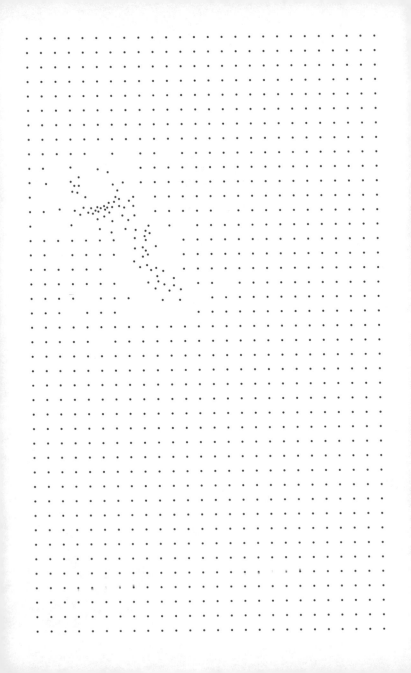

3: the re-emergence of culture after the mass-age

Society comes together around culture. It is what we share. And it's not just culture in the singular. Rather, we exist in many cultures, interlaced and overlapping, made up of belief systems, interests, and values. Culture is made meaningful through the language of art: poetry, song, color, film, dance, ritual. These are the ways we express our culture and how we maintain a filament of connection to others.

The Mass-Age transformed culture by providing massive and global cultural narratives. The star of the Mass-Age was The Brand: a business idea with cultural influence—think Nike, Coke, Pepsi, Apple, or IBM. It was so successful, it led to branded politics (Red vs. Blue) and branded individuals (the power of your personal brand). Mass media begat mass brands and the most powerful of them initiated, and were pivotal to, influential cultural concepts, conversations about humanity that cohered us into large groups, or to use marketing parlance, segments.

The Mass-Age loved polarities: winners or losers, up or down, success or failure, belonging or loneliness, right or left, Christian or Muslim, good or evil, right or wrong. The list goes on and on. Polarities create big segments, big enough to market to on a large scale, big enough to make democracy appear simple. Yet throughout all this were complexities, cultural diversities in all walks of life and across the whole spectrum—not just monochrome—ideas, ideologies, and hypotheses of human life. Mass culture in the

Mass-Age aspired to unanimity. The Beatles got it right; the aspiration of the Mass-Age was to a life where "all you need is love," and it still may be, but the journey to that higher realization takes us through many conflicts, many ancient differences, and many experiences. Aspiring to "one love" is possible only if you acknowledge that, though there may be one love, there are a multitude of cultural values and human experiences to be reconciled. The Mass-Age attempted this reconciliation with endless images of "humanity" all contrived by Western media to conform to a story of powerful and powerless, rich and poor, advanced and emerging, and again, on and on and on. In the Mass-Age, Western media attempted to impose a cultural hegemony on the world.

It has failed. As the Mass-Age fades, the incredible diversity of our human expressions—our identities and our experiences—are revealed. Culture is more robust than we thought. Young people across the world are mining their cultural history for meaning, and culture itself has proved to be a formidable adversary to the mechanized atrocity of the mass market. Culture is identity. It is how we belong, how we simplify the world so as to relate to it. Culture is our meaning. Looking out from where you are, you can see many cultures, many meanings, many truths, many priorities, many skepticisms, many colors, many obsessions. Many—not one. Not a single mass, but a multitude. Not unity, but diversity. Conversations between people are conversations between, not across, cultures. Culture is more powerful, more present, and more dangerous than it has ever been, because it represents who we are and how we make meaning of the world.

It is worth having a look at systems we relied on during the Mass-Age, one of which was the social sciences. The essence of science—social or otherwise—is that an experiment can be repeated to produce a predictable response. The problem is, social sciences simply cannot do that, not really. To quote physicist Richard Feynman, "Social science is an example of a science which is not a science. They follow the forms. (They) gather data, (they) do so-and-so and so forth, but they don't get any laws, they haven't found out anything."

Think about it: If social sciences *could* produce a predictable result, we would not have been surprised as a whole in the 2016 elections—in the U.K. with Brexit and in the U.S. with Trump. On both sides of the pond, the pollsters didn't see it coming. They did not predict anything. And they never can. The social scientist, at some level, has subjectively designed a questionnaire. Of course, many social scientists would disagree with that statement. There are also behavioral scientists who are now equipped with the ability to track real behavior—not reported behavior or reported perspectives, attitudes, and prejudices. But the idea that a piece of data about human behavior is absolutely predictable, as science expects it to be, is dangerous. It is an observation, and because it takes a long time to do the work that social scientists like to do, they are often too late to the conversation. You do not need social science to believe that the eagle should be a protected species or that women should have equal rights under the law.

One of the sickest moments of the Mass-Age was the denial by seven tobacco-industry CEOs who said they saw no correlation (note the word *correlation*) between smoking and cancer. Even today those with a self-interest, such as Rex Tillerson's Exxon Mobil, spend millions of dollars corrupting the view of climate change in order to deny the role played by burning fossil fuels. The degradation of our planet has long been observed by indigenous cultures, by individuals, and by communities across the world. Communities of mountain climbers and skiers have, through their own cultural conversations, been lamenting global warming for decades. Inuit culture is being threatened by climate change. All of which is to say this: Observing the world through the lens of social science-style research will fail you. The imperative for anyone who wants to engage with the world is to engage through and with culture. This means we need to elevate the people with cultural skills to the same level as everyone else in business and politics.

During the Mass-Age, we elevated the social sciences to something of a belief system in the U.S. But our last presidential election told a different story. In a *New Republic* article titled "Thanks, Trump! What He Got Right About American Democracy," Kevin Baker writes:

> *The big question that remains from the 2016 campaign is not how Trump could get it so right. It's how all the professionals who have taken over our political system—the consultants and pollsters, the opposition researchers and social media savants, the phone-bank organizers and fund-raising planners, the ad buyers and copywriters and media analysts—could get it so wrong.*

Donald Trump did not use social science. His campaign did not concern itself with focus groups and surveys and telephone canvasing. He used big data, but he used it as pertaining to social media—

and social media is *not* social science. It is culture. During the Mass-Age, our democracy was managed by mass media and social science, and our politicians could not listen with clarity to the nature of democracy, the nature of politics; politics is all culture, all the time. The attitudes, the fears, the hopes... politicians could not hear accurately because they were using the tools of the social sciences to listen to their electorate. Donald Trump did not use these tools. As Baker put it, "Trump was the first purely *instinctual* presidential candidate we have seen in a long, long time... a man self-taught in all the elements of the modern political campaign: how to read what the customer wants, and command the camera, and look like a winner."

Consider the ways in which candidates used media in the Mass-Age, be it Roosevelt and his fireside radio chats, or Kennedy's use of home movies, Reagan's use of commercial television, Bill Clinton's use of late-night talk shows and MTV, and now, Donald Trump's use of Twitter. For better or worse, Trump wielded a creative person's instinct to gain attention. It was a massive jolt to the system and, arguably, the moment the Mass-Age ended. From that point on, the question was not: How do I target millennials? The question became: What are the core values of the culture? How does this culture think? What does it care about? How does it feel? How can it express itself? How do I become part of it? How can my culture co-create society with other cultures? This style of inquiry is purely narrative engagement and listening, and it cannot be done through the mechanism of social science. It is a creative experience—a cultural experience.

This approach is informed intuition based on deep connectivity to human nature, and I believe you change the world not through reason but through intuition. Several of my friends expected Trump's victory based upon their understanding of culture. They were obviously hearing things that our establishment and our mainstream media were not. They were at the fringe, and fringe culture is full of alternative narratives. Trump was successful where others failed; he broke a Mass-Age hegemony. By contrast, consider Barack Obama. He was a mass-market president. He understood how to engender balance. He was erudite and thoughtful and did not seek to create a divide or tension. His point of view was to unify the mass. President Trump does not employ the same strategy, and in doing so he tore open the conversation, revealing the *cultural* conversation. The one we want to have, we need to have. The one that will lead to a new narrative.

Marketing has once again taken a cue from politics after the Mass-Age. Nike was among the early adopters. They understood the culture of sports and athletes, and developed social justice campaigns, making efforts to empower women in Majority World regions and implement environmental controls in its business operations. In recognizing the congruence between a clean world, healthy athletes, and gender and racial equality, the company made the celebration of fairness and competition an organic cultural journey. In building desire for their products and services, they pivoted from the social science that was failing other companies. They understood the value of engaging deeply in the culture of sports and its varied communities.

All of which is to say that the study of culture now, after the Mass-Age, is a more profound way of learning about people than what we were offered by social scientists. I do not claim the field is entirely bunk. The goal of its honest practitioners is laudable. But I believe our reliance on one single mode of learning has tripped up both our democracy and our industries. While some of these Mass-Age tools have truly helped us describe people, it is worth noting that over the past decade, the capacity for market research, in particular, to help us make sound decisions has diminished. Some firms can no longer provide the actionable intelligence that clients need to understand their audience. The customer might be defined in some way that suits a system, but it does not mean you understand them.

We must now augment these Mass-Age tools with meaningful cultural insight. We must be respectful of, and engaged with, culture, and that demands we also know what culture is. In general, businesspeople don't really know where to start. Many people are quick to mention religion, but culture is not only that.

During the Mass-Age, and the Industrial Age that created it, cultural values were suppressed. They are now bursting forth in all their anarchic glory—not because they are new but because they're actually old, and they have found a mode of public expression and coherence. Media and culture have always been inextricably linked. When we see a media transformation, we will see a cultural transformation. It is exciting to witness culture transformed from its domination by mass experiences into a collection of smaller ones, experiences that are more meaningful to the individual.

A good example of this occurred to me when in Dhaka, Bangladesh, during the Egyptian uprising. Just north of Dhaka, half-naked people scrambled across the hulks of decommissioned steel ships, salvaging and recycling the metal. In the city is a music subculture that is connected to both Japan and Norway, clubs that host death metal bands as they travel from the Northern to the Southern Hemisphere. How do you tell *that* story? How does it help you understand the world, your market, and your consumer?

The same group of photography students who told me about the death metal clubs reported that they were excited to see the American-backed dictator be removed from office in Egypt by their fellow millennial Muslims. This is a completely different narrative from the one expressed in Western media. We need both and all narratives. Each is a fragment, part of a whole, part of a pattern. These are complex narratives that knit together complex histories and contexts. The mass media would have a singular story: Egypt liberated by freedom fighters empowered by Western technology. Or Dhaka as a struggling economy reliant on a garment industry serving Western needs. In the Mass-Age, such cultures were subservient to Western cultures, but now the opposite is true: Cultures are dynamic. People are able to access and borrow from the global cultural kaleidoscope—creating new experiences, absorbing and projecting new values and new ideas, taking and giving inspiration.

After the Mass-Age, culture is the primary means by which we will navigate our future. Technology and science will create amazing opportunities, none of which we will be able to embrace if we do not understand the world and the people we need to relate to. The biggest threat to our success is ignorance. The Mass-Age made ignorance bliss. Those days are over, and we must now do the fascinating and difficult work of embracing the experience of unknowing and evolve our own cultural identities as businesses, as organizations, and of course, as individuals. ▲

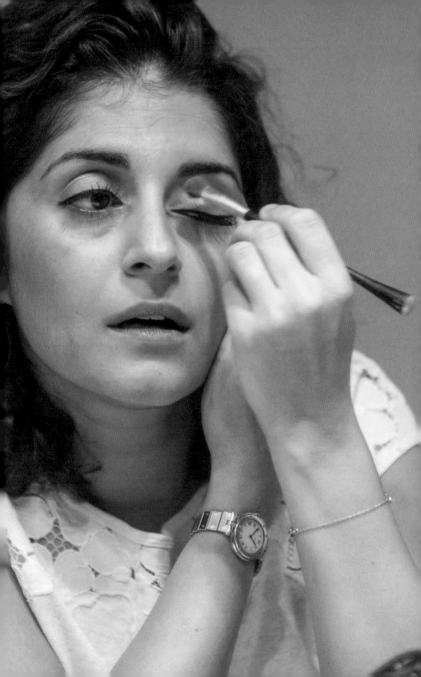

SENSATION YOUNG BRITISH ARTISTS FROM THE SAATCHI COLLECTION

DEAD CHILDREN PLAYING A Picture Book by Stanley Donwood & Dr. Tchock

Outsiders Compiled by Steve Lazarides

richard prince american prayer · bibliothèque nationale de france · gagosian gallery

SPECTOR RICHARD PRINCE Guggenheim

DREAM STEPHANIE CHERNIKOWSKI 2.13.61

MAN MARK ROTHKO The Solomon R. Guggenheim Museum / Abrams

david salle gagosian gallery

NN SOME KINDA VOCATION

THE ART OF GETTING OVER *StephenPowers* ST. MARTIN'S PRESS

THE ART OF GILBERT AND GEORGE BY WOLF JAHN · Thames and Hudson

ndida Ryan McGinness Studio Franchise Estudio franquicia

9 788496 917637

VE

AN MCGINNESS vocabularytest JOSEPhSILVESTROGALLERY

n McGinness ks. R

John Baldessari Deutsche Guggenheim

ཨོཾ་ཨཱཿཧཱུྃ་བཛྲ་གུ་རུ་པདྨ་སིདྡྷི་ཧཱུྃ

HOUSTON

BALDESSARI RE UTY

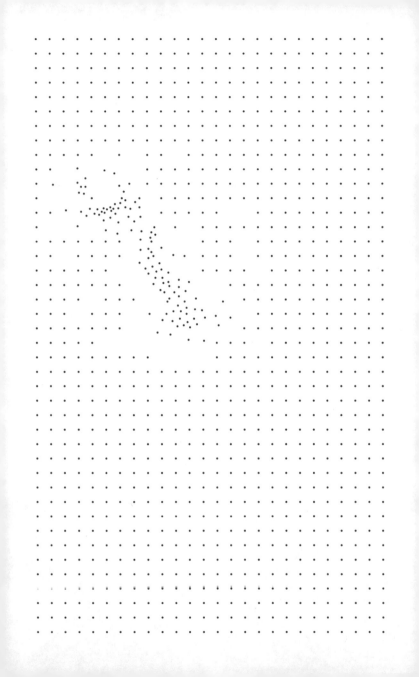

4: the nature of leadership after the mass-age

Leadership—as an art form, as a social action, and as a strategy—is being challenged. The Mass-Age created a context within which leadership came from the top of a human pyramid, a Maslovian model that imbued leaders with magical powers to inspire, articulate, and move forward with the plan that the mass would follow. The perfect sound bite, the photo opportunity, and the thirty-second commercial—those were the tools of leadership. In business, the ability to inspire, to create in others the desired action, is seen as an admirable quality. Leadership has been the outer projection of an inner narrative, a vision and a direction offered to a community.

Leadership came from the top, and in the Western model it came from the individual. Businesses still need strategies, goals, and an organizational plan to get there. After the Mass-Age, things get more complicated. After the Mass-Age, a network is more powerful than a hierarchy, and new forms of leadership are emerging. Leadership is not only about explaining the strategy; it is about engaging the network in both creating the strategy and in executing it. The qualities we admire in a leader are shifting, and they incorporate new and very powerful ideas. These are ideas of: listening to the other; leading a conversation; developing and articulating a narrative of inclusion rather than instruction; and inspiring because the leader reflects the values and aspirations of the followers.

Returning to the political context, we just witnessed a German election in which the right wing experienced a resurgence. But in the German electoral system, the leader has to build a coalition. It is a multi-party model, voted on by proportional representation, which is anathema to the systems of the U.K. and U.S. In summer 2017, Emmanuel Macron proposed such reform in France, away from a polarized model to a pluralized one. So, what does it mean? In this proportional system, leadership becomes about cohering different groups— smaller but numerous political parties, public referenda and open voting (for both candidates *and* parties), and multi-member districts—to a common goal. For Macron in France, the ultimate goal is the transformation of France's democracy, one encouraged by a variety of voices and fairness otherwise stifled by a binary approach. Although evolved in the Mass-Age, proportional representation is well equipped for the new reality. In a polarized system, the minority is suppressed; in a pluralized system, the minority is acknowledged. Thus compromise and discussion become necessary by the very nature of this more complex system. Leadership becomes about listening and leading conversations that enable coherent narratives to emerge. Consensus is not bland and useless compromise; it becomes a pivotal act of leadership.

One could argue that proportional representation is a good model for how the future could be everywhere, that after the Mass-Age it will be more important to understand the many cultures we must engage with and how we can lead them. And the way to lead multiple narratives with diverse values is not through dictatorial direction. It is not about a homogenous consistency in stated values, which does little more than drive people to write mission statements that are meaningless—ultimately anodyne gestures prompted by the idea of getting everybody to agree to something.

Instead, this atmosphere of competing perspectives sets up a tension that effective leadership must recognize and resolve. To ease this tension, we must resolve moral dilemmas, resolve conflict, and resolve intellectual disagreement. This leadership can cohere people around goals but then be open to as-yet-unknown ways of reaching those goals. People need not agree, but their opinions must stem from a common goal, not the corporate noise and optics that so often drown it.

A great example of a conflict based on spurious polarities is the conflict around climate change, and the lack of wholesale agreement about the need to regulate carbon emissions. We are stuck in a polarity that pits science against religion and societal good against individual aspiration. None of these polarities is relevant. We need to regulate carbon emissions because our home, the planet, is being destroyed by them. We have yet to see leadership that can knit people with different experiences and beliefs into this common pursuit. Agents of self-interest, and the corruption of politics by money, have effectively denied access to good conversation. In this transition from Mass-Age communication and political strategy, we need new leadership that does not emanate from old polarities. A coalition could be created between interested parties: workers who stand to lose economically, religious people who are opposed to the denial of God's work, and the governors of both state and nation. The conversation need not deny divine purpose, need not deny the economic challenges of working people, or even the profit and aspiration of business. South Africa emerged from apartheid through the power of the conversational leadership skills of Nelson Mandela. In this post-Mass-Age world, these are the leadership skills we could aspire to.

Take Uber. After their assorted public relations fiascos, newly installed CEO Dara Khosrowshahi observed a fundamental lack of awareness. "This company has to change," he said. "What got us here is not what's going to get us to the next level." In a September 2017 email to employees, Khosrowshahi wrote, "It really matters what people think of us, especially in a global business like ours, where actions in one part of the world can have serious consequences in another. Going forward, it's critical that we act with integrity in everything we do, and learn how to be a better partner to every city we operate in." Khosrowshahi saw that the real problem was not Uber's corporate mission statement or literature; these were flawed and ineffective anyway. The problem was the nature of its leadership.

Many of us act, we do things, but we don't really understand why—that is, until we get to a place of meaning. Meaning is a journey, and we get there through discussion, involvement, and experience. Meaning happens through truths, not facts—and those truths are found through stories. In my work, I have begun to understand that what I do and the reason I do it is to help people get somewhere, and that is not top-down leadership. It is, instead, being a guide. It's facilitation It is: Where do you need to go? Let me see if I can help you get there. Let's talk and find our way to the real problem—and its solution—together. And that takes more than whiteboards or Post-its or even a mission statement.

First, to provide guidance, one must have clarity about what it is to be accomplished, which entails picking through ideas, goals, stories, and cultures. The process entails discipline and the ability to be immersed in a complex conversation but then establish structure. This involves organizing thoughts into a piece of meaningful communication.

Second, if I walk into a room, I can do so either as an ignorant or knowledgeable party, and adjust the balance of both. Sometimes it is quite useful to approach a moment uninformed and without fear of the unknown. Dumb questions can open up good conversations. In a world of assumptions and prejudice, they can help people realize there are basic questions that need to be answered.

In my work, the third element is knowledge. It could be knowledge about social trends. It could be economic knowledge. Knowledge is information plus meaning. Knowledge is created, not found; it exists within relationships and across communities. Knowledge is not facts. Knowledge emerges from narrative. Knowledge is the product of community, and the language of community is art. In other words, how we tell the story, how we craft the image, how we represent the data—all are huge elements of the narrative that coheres community. Leadership after the Mass-Age is returning to its roots as a projection of shared narrative. Leadership is a cultural discipline, not a military one. The community that shares narrative is strong, directed, and successful. The community with no shared narrative declines into dust.

Creative professionals have insights about the world at their fingertips; they can help clients make good decisions. And when every piece of information has a hundred stories, we must also know how to synthesize this knowledge in a way that is meaningful to a business and its strategy. Thoughtful discipline, generative questions, and culture-based research bring this meaning—the story—together. As a guide, everything is about narrative. And narrative after the Mass-Age is not top-down. Leadership after the Mass-Age is not top-down. Both are rooted in conversations and conversational leadership.

Businesses must learn the art of conversational leadership. Take the newest head of Microsoft, Satya Nadella. In a 2017 interview with Nadella, NPR's Aarti Shahani reported that his ability to empathize "becomes key as he looks at those Microsoft workers who are pointing fingers." Nadella described how his instinct is to judge or be annoyed. Instead, "he pulls back and remembers they're complaining because they're hungry to do more. And it's his job to give them hope."

Nadella recognized his responsibility as facilitator and guide. In February 2017, he told *USA Today*, "It's so critical for leaders not to freak people out, but to give them air cover to solve the real problem. If people are doing things out of fear, it's hard or impossible to actually drive any innovation."

It is worth noting that Nadella grew up in India. An immigrant to the U.S. now leads one of the top three most highly valued brands on the planet, and in doing so has brought different cultural values to the company.

Western norms are increasingly being challenged after the Mass-Age. Contrast the

command-and-control mindset of our Western
DNA with give-and-take power structures—
networked paths of soft power, where instead
of influence manifested through wealth or force,
it may be shown through social connections or
even mysticism.

Japan is another example. Honda's *waigaya*
conversational tool is oft cited for its free flow of
ideas and constant pushback against the status quo.
The model of leadership has shifted dramatically,
from that of a manufacturing approach to a
network based on relationships, cooperation, and
ultimately, community.

Former Microsoft CEO Steve Ballmer practiced
a closed mentality in business. For example, Ballmer,
when showed the first iPhone back in 2007, ridiculed
it on television. He laughed at its high price tag and
said it wouldn't appeal to email-dependent business
customers because it did not have a physical keyboard.
He was so certain of this, he smirked his way through
the interview. That was Ballmer's leadership. During
his fourteen-year tenure, the company's stock value
flatlined. Microsoft's cultural cachet faded into
irrelevance as tech companies like Facebook, Google,
and Apple excelled in their respective arenas, with
soaring market caps.

Fast forward to 2015, when his successor, Satya
Nadella, walked onstage at a tech conference with
an iPhone. He projects an image of an iPhone home
screen—but to show how many of its applications in
fact originated at Microsoft. This cross-pollination of
advances would not be possible without a collaborative
industry. None of these technologies exists without
massive collaborative efforts and negotiations.
By acknowledging these human relationships, by

celebrating them, Nadella is redefining the ability of Microsoft to lead.

And Nadella is *open* to the idea that Microsoft can be a leading player in one field and a following player in another. He was open to the idea that the iPhone is better than the product made by his company, and given that reality, Microsoft should stop making their product. He laid off 18,000 people based on this decision to preserve the jobs of 100,000 others. But his pivotal insight was that Microsoft was not the right company to make phones. It should be somebody else, and Microsoft should collaborate with that somebody else, be it Samsung or Apple or whomever.

In 2017, I attended an event honoring architect and placemaker Donald J. Stastny, noted for his civic contributions in urban planning. Throughout the presentation, hosted by the Architecture Foundation of Oregon, Stastny was rightly hailed as a leader, but what resonated with me was how his leadership was emphasized as a *service*. I considered how this amazingly successful man with strong character and, presumably, ego understood the difficult conversations—creative, social, and political in scope—required to create public works of meaning and monument. He knew how to facilitate truthful dialogues. This is exactly the leadership I believe is vital after the Mass-Age.

Leadership *is* service, and service begins with listening. Leaders facilitate voices coming together with other voices to identify the real problem, and design a solution. Leaders are here to encourage an open flow of ideas and stories. Leaders are here to help communities find narrative and open the opportunity for change. Leadership can be a creative process. Steve Jobs always understood this. The story was as important as the strategy. In the first three minutes of his iconic 2007 presentation of the iPhone, he won. He won with a story well told. It was brave. It did not fall into a market view. He *created* a market view and brought all his skills to bear on imagining an easy-to-use product that put the power of the internet into our hands. In effect, his story was the story of human evolution. The most powerful innovation in recent history, the internet, once the sole domain of elites, was placed into the hands of everyone. He was right. He made history. His story.

Leadership after the Mass-Age embraces new skills of conversational leadership, new skills of listening to the other, and new skills of organizing often disparate groups, creating community with shared narrative.

Creative work, the work of storytellers and image makers, is essential to leadership. Art and science are the yin and yang of this story; they need each other, and leadership is challenged to integrate them into coherent community narratives that do, in fact, change the world. ▲

superpoze

gaîté lyriqu

— 26 nov

baghir

Visions

Verniссage le 2 décembre 2015
à partir de 19h en présence de l'artiste

Galerie Photo 12
14, rue des Jardins Saint-Paul
75004 Paris
galerie@galerie-photo12.com
+ 33 (0) 1 42 78 24 21

Exposition
du 3 décembre 2015 au 16 janvier 2016

Du mardi au dimanche de 14h à 18h30
et nocturne tous les jeudi jusqu'à 23h

www.baghir.com
baghir@baghir.com

Baghir

Visions

Verniссage le 2 décembre 2015
à partir de 19h en présence de l'artiste

Galerie Photo 12
14, rue des Jardins Saint-Paul
75004 Paris
galerie@galerie-photo12.com
+ 33 (0) 1 42 78 24 21

Exposition
du 3 décembre 201

Du mardi au diman
et nocturne tous les

www.baghir.com
baghir@baghir.com

OE GOSS

SIVITÉ AU PRINTEMPS

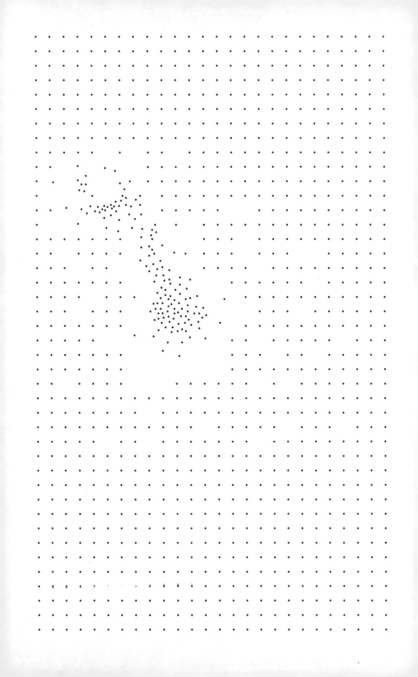

5: the role of creative collaboration after the mass-age

During the Mass-Age, industrial structure found its way into all aspects of life—and profoundly reorganized the way humanity worked. The crowning glory of the Industrial Age—the factory—was grounded in the innovative concept that any human or mechanical process could be broken down into its constituent factors, understood at that level, and replicated to produce at scale.

Industrialized thinking and the process of factorization did not end with the manufacturing of goods and the refinement of processes. Industrialized thinking also made its way into the social sciences, underpinning its practitioners' attempts to factorize the human experience, and to understand its constituent parts in order to explain human behavior. Using social science research, marketers have attempted to factorize consumer behavior for over half a century. The creation of ideas became an industrial process in and of itself. The most successful companies of the early days of the Mass-Age—Coca-Cola, Procter & Gamble, General Motors—were those companies who migrated their industrial expertise to the task of creating culturally influential ideas.

These companies became market leaders in the Mass-Age by creating what we now call "brands." The way they created brands was to mass-produce emotional connections, using television as a lead medium. Television created a mass audience, and, if you could command television, you could create mass emotional attachment. It was a command-and-control system, in which advertising was incredibly effective in the hands of marketers who had complete control over the presentation, including distribution and pricing, of their products and services. Advertising in the Mass-Age could focus on one factor—the emotional engagement of a consumer—though other factors also had to be in place and controlled effectively: where the consumer came across the product, their experience of buying the product, and their experience of using it. Branding is a multidisciplinary activity that proved amazingly powerful in the Mass-Age, when done well.

Coca-Cola, Procter & Gamble, and General Motors started to decline as the Mass-Age came to its end. Once the process of factorization was achieved, it could be copied. The kind of emotional appeals made by brands at the height of the Mass-Age were made possible because the marketer controlled the means of distribution, not only of the products and services they offered, but the messages and ideas they disseminated. Controlling a mass medium is relatively simple; it takes power, and in the Mass-Age, power was money. The pinnacle of Mass-Age media was the Super Bowl in the U.S. If you had the money to hire the best advertising agency and pay the cost of a thirty-second spot, at a price tag of about four million dollars, then you could command the attention of an audience of over 100 million people. At the peak of the Mass-Age, the audience had no other media. It was a rapt audience. Nike benefited from this rapt audience of sports fans, as did Budweiser and its frogs. Even Apple, launching the Macintosh in 1984 and teasing the iPhone in 2007, could take advantage of the captive television audience delivered by the Super Bowl. But as the Mass-Age came to an end, the audience was less rapt—and a new reality emerged.

Specifically, what has come to its end is the ability to control the distribution of ideas. As soon as this control was lost, influence was lost. The scale of the Super Bowl audience is probably the same, but the power of the telecast's commercials is undeniably less. There must be complete congruence between the ideals of the consumer and the ideals of the corporation for such advertising to work today. Wieden+Kennedy's 2011 Super Bowl commercial for the Chrysler 500 was one such moment of congruence. It was a commercial for a car, but it was also a new narrative for the city of Detroit, the Chrysler company, its workers, and its aspirations. The commercial presented the idea of quality as a cultural aspiration grounded in the hard work, industrial prowess, and mettle of the city's workers.

Media control has been lost because there are now an infinite number of channels available to the individual. Television still has the power to create an emotional appeal, but the audience absorbs multiple competing narratives. The challenge for a post-Mass-Age marketer in both the commercial and political realms is to achieve congruence. Without congruence, the audience is at best skeptical, often cynical, and—most worryingly for marketers—senses a brand's lack of integrity and its self-orientation. This ultimately leads to an absence of trust. Brands today are often simply unbelievable.

The tools of the Mass-Age—polling, focus groups, and market segmentations—are failing because they are techniques of generalities that fail to illuminate the human condition. It is no accident that two of the most powerful brands at the end of the Mass-Age, Nike and Apple, eschew such techniques in favor of elevating the creative process, the creative mind, and the ability of the artist to understand and tell the truth of the human condition. This is how congruence occurs, and it demands a fundamental shift in the way business and politics relate to the world.

The Mass-Age saw the rise of the social science-based tools that defined learning and became the controlling factors in communication. Yet even in the Mass-Age, breakthrough inspiration came from creative people who were able to break free from the constraints of polling, of focus groups, and of "marketing" as it became defined. Bill Backer, who originated the idea "I'd like to buy the world a Coke"; Hal Riney, who wrote "Morning in America" for Ronald Reagan; Dan Wieden, who wrote "Just do it" for Nike; Lee Clow, who supervised Apple's "1984" commercial and the artistry of Apple's iPod "Silhouettes" and "Mac vs. PC" campaigns—these professionals were (and are) creative people, artists in their practice. Their learning was a creative process, informed by information, data, and their own collaborations with their audiences, their clients, their team, and the people who made the work. As the Mass-Age reached its zenith, this was a rare achievement. Nearly everywhere else, the process by such people was replaced by data, analytics, and a form of strategy that assumed humans were metrics to be moved. Apple did the opposite. Apple learned through artists, and the result was that its advertising moved hearts, moved minds, and moved mountains of iPods, Macs, and iPhones.

Over the years, I have had personal experiences of intense and extraordinary collaborations.

Wieden+Kennedy, the advertising agency for which I was the lead strategist in the nineties, amassed many experiences of collaboration in the creation of great advertising: with Joe Pytka, the commercials director, for example; between Jim Riswold, copywriter and creative director, and Tinker Hatfield, the creator of the Air Jordan shoe; with Spike Lee and, of course, with Michael Jordan himself; with David Bowie, who gave us a master class in leading a collaboration when he asked us to help strategize his return to popular music with his album *Black Tie White Noise*; with Brian Eno on the creation of the boot-up sound of Windows 95; and between the agency and the people of ESPN to create SportsCenter advertising. These are just a few examples, and in each example there were smart, confident, and creative minds working collaboratively within a clear structure and with strong leadership.

These experiences had a huge effect on the way I thought about the management of the creative process itself. I found that Brian Eno runs his business, as did David Bowie, structured so that the artist can be a generous partner in his collaborators' thinking. When you work with Eno, there is always humor, and sure, a sort of rock-star thing in effect, but the end result is deep thought and real collaboration. And as with Bowie, this productivity owes much to a relational management structure. The discipline, the deadlines, the finances—these daily realities are grounded in rock-solid, established partnerships, which thereby liberate the artist to be truly, profoundly collaborative.

Take, for example, how David Bowie made his final masterpiece, 2016's *Blackstar*. He had already written the lyrics, he knew the melody, but it wasn't orchestrated yet. He was searching for the music.

And then he heard it in a bar in Greenwich Village, being performed by a jazz group helmed by saxophonist Donny McCaslin. He soon invited McCaslin and company into the studio, into the process of his collaborative leadership. "He set the tone from the beginning," McCaslin told *The Guardian*. "He told us: 'Whatever you hear, I want you to go with it.' He said 'great' to everything."

The best musicians are exemplars in understanding the fluid relationships between leadership and collaboration. Robert Plant is such an example. His creative process throughout the years has incorporated sonic reference points from all manner of American, Celtic, Middle Eastern, and African cultures. In a 2014 *New York Times* story, guitarist Justin Adams described Plant as both a leader and catalyst in an incredible interplay of musicianship:

> *With all of those years of experience, it's not like he's learned a huge amount of complex music theory. But he has learned a lot of complex vibe management. He can create an atmosphere where suddenly lightning is more likely to strike. In collaborative music, it's often not a question of careful writing and composition and all these sorts of things. It's more the spirit of the moment when things come together in a flash.*

The essence of music is collaboration. It's an intoxicating circle. And that is also how we need to perceive leadership now. Instead of leading from the top down, leaders need to cultivate the art of complex vibe management. Even the greatest orchestral conductor is working to get the most out of his or her musicians. We need leadership that serves collaboration—with different groups coming together, listening, contributing, and creating something together, something new. That is the creative process. That's David Bowie working with the jazz group. That's David Bowie working with Nile Rodgers. That's Brian Eno working with Talking Heads and Laurie Anderson and John Cale. That's George Harrison, John Lennon, Ringo Starr, and Paul McCartney meeting Ravi Shankar. That's Philip Glass meeting Ravi Shankar. That's Dr. Dre meeting Jimmy Iovine. That's Dr. Dre meeting Eminem. That's Miles Davis meeting Teo Macero. That's the entire business model of Supreme. This is the creativity of art, of culture, and it is essential after the Mass-Age. The fundamental shift we need is to embrace and evolve new skills of collaboration.

Currently, business collaboration is often a cliché mask for a brainstorm. Collaboration is a highly disciplined process, with effective and inspirational leadership. It is a creative process, not a military one. It is a way of listening and learning as well as designing and making. The reason we can look to musicians, artists, and athletes for instruction is that the skills of collaboration are essential in those enterprises. Many stage actors talk about how their relationship with the audience is what energizes a great performance. Athletes talk of the energy exchange between the fans and their performance. Writers talk about really knowing their reader, almost personally, and writing for her. Dan Wieden used to have a photo of Steve Prefontaine above his typewriter. He wrote for Pre. All these energetic exchanges are the stuff of collaboration, the fact of generative creativity and innovation. It is the energy that was created between Lee Clow's team at Chiat/Day and Steve Jobs' team at Apple. It was the energy between Nike's marketers and their agency team at Wieden+Kennedy. These kinds of collaboration were disciplined and led effectively, and yet the collaborators were able to learn quickly, share, and hybridize ideas. These collaborations emerged at the end of the Mass-Age, and today they offer insight into the skills we need in the unregulated, culturally chaotic world of the digital age, where we are impervious to linear cause and effect. The post-Mass-Age balances the power of analytics and social science with the extraordinary power of creative insight and collaborative leadership.

With this creativity as an imperative, we can no longer approach business as a military command-and-control operation, but approach it as a network. It functions on fundamentally different human values. In the network realm, I have to work with another person, and I have to not only contribute to their work but have them contribute to mine. The operating principle is generosity. Mass-Age companies like Coca-Cola, Procter & Gamble, and Boeing were products of an engineering world, where collaboration meant something completely different. In the post-Mass-Age world, collaboration not only means bringing different skills together to solve problems, like engineers do, but collaborating creatively by sharing inspirations, listening, changing, and being guided by common aspirations, motivations, and goals.

Satya Nadella, newly appointed CEO of Microsoft, an Industrial Age software behemoth, is reinvigorating the sleeping giant by focusing on a powerful truth: "Our industry does not respect tradition—it only respects innovation."

Yes, yes, and yes. Tradition is a powerful cultural energy, but it is the antithesis of collaboration in modern organizations after the Mass-Age. To adopt the traditional way of bringing insight to market is, as they say, to bring a knife to a gunfight. Innovation is a creative process; it emerges from well-led collaborations that are amazingly effective when the community of collaborators is inspired to achieve a goal. The open-source movement is abundant with values that elevate collaboration, decry self-orientation, and establish highly disciplined modes of working. Nadella also believes that work has to be meaningful, and has to improve people's lives. This is obviously true in the broadest sense, but it is now true in a managerial sense. Nadella sees his role as a leader of a company that needs to collaborate on a massive scale. He sees his leadership as a tool for that collaboration, to enable emergence and improve the lives of people at Microsoft, of the very people with whom he needs to create and collaborate in order to reboot the corporation as an innovative organization. He is an agent of cultural change who prioritizes the joy of contribution over the satisfaction of winning.

When we consider marketing, communications, branding, and cultural conversations, there is no work anymore without collaboration. The concept is so ubiquitous it has become a buzzword. But it's not about brainstorming or getting together for an offsite meeting. Underneath the buzzword is a discipline. Collaboration must be led, and it must be led by a creative thinker, because creative thinkers are multidisciplinary. They have imaginations. And, as Albert Einstein said, "Imagination is more important than knowledge. For knowledge is limited, whereas imagination embraces the entire world, stimulating progress, giving birth to evolution."

Collaboration teaches us something. Whereas the industrial Mass-Age formalized the imperial power of a command-and-control mode of thought, we now work with a Majority World in which success comes from collaboration. The shift—the friction—is deeper than it looks at first. We feel the resulting tension in our current politics, economic systems, and global relationships. We can liken this period to a butterfly coming out of its chrysalis: It's an ugly, deformed creature that doesn't quite work until a beautiful, functional unit emerges and learns to fly. This is where we are.

We are being birthed into this new world, newly open, where in order to thrive we must collaborate. Where we must accept others and listen. Where mutual respect is essential. Where we have to cooperate. Where we learn *from* others, not *about* them. Where we allow such learning to change us. Where we end the conversations that get us stuck in old modes, and we instead embrace new conversations that take us into the unknown, perhaps even into a place of fear and discomfort. This is not where we are today. We are in the unknown. The old ways have not prepared us for this. Our creative people—our writers, designers, art directors, imagineers, and performers—know this place well. It is the blank page, the curtain rising, or the whistle blowing. What happens next is up to you.

Nicholas Humphrey's 2003 book *The Inner Eye* offers a social reexamination of Darwin's evolutionary theory. Darwin's theory—that the fittest survive—has been lodged in America's culture for generations, and has underpinned American society and the capitalist ethos. The most successful are the ones who win in this zero-sum dynamic. But Humphrey claims otherwise; he argues persuasively that another reading of Darwin's famous theory posits that many successful evolutions did not actually occur through competition, but through cooperation. Competition is not the only engine of evolution. Cooperation is one of the means by which *Homo sapiens* became the apex predator of the world.

We are at a pivotal moment in humanity. Competition—part and parcel of a command-and-control scenario—has led us to where we are, but cooperation and collaboration within social networks will take us to a different place. Admittedly, this presents new problems, but it still marks a revolutionary change. Nobody will listen to your command, and control is not yours to have. Thus, if you are to participate in any creative work, if you are in business or in politics—if you are to engage and thrive in this perpetually networked world—after the Mass-Age, the mode of operation must be a fully conscious collaboration. It must be web-led by people who are open to feeling vulnerable and excited by the unknowingness of it. These are characteristics of creative people. We need them in our deliberations, our strategizing, our learning, and our decision-making.

From a historic perspective, and from the perspective of interest in global markets, the Mass-Age was the culmination of the move to industrialization. It was, in effect, the cultural consequence of industrial-powered imperialism. In the hegemony, the means of cultural production were controlled by Western corporations that viewed the "third world" as nothing more than emerging markets and a cheap labor supply. The digital and social technology revolutions combined to destroy this old imperial power structure, accelerating the economic growth of the Majority World and altering the distribution of influence. By placing the means of cultural production in the hands of *everyone*, culture itself was unleashed on the world.

In the Mass-Age, ancient and local cultural ideas or values were suppressed by mass media's need for a homogenized consumer culture oriented to material aspiration and Maslow's view of self-actualization. But Maslow himself was a Western Christian, who channeled Western philosophical traditions into social science models of consumer behavior and attitudes. He was, in effect, only right for his own culture. Self-actualization is not related to material comfort in the Majority World. The extraordinary work of Ronald Inglehart and Christian Welzel over the last forty years has painted one of the truest social science-based pictures of the world: a world on a journey to openness and secularity as a means of liberating local cultures and individual identities within a framework of economic advancement. Along the way, the tensions between the older closed ways of being and the newer more open ways caused conflict. The Mass-Age, a mere fifty years from McCluhan's *The Medium Is the Massage* to the present day, suppressed these conflicts with a veneer of material aspiration within a consumer culture literally broadcast from the West to the Rest. These conflicts are now emerging, unleashed by the unregulated and uncontrolled power shift of social media. The medium was indeed the Mass-Age, but now it is the social network. Alongside the extraordinary economic shifts made possible by information technology and manufacturing advancements, we see a new imperative.

As mass media fragmented, trust in mass institutions declined, from political parties and governments to brands and corporations. Money corrupted all, and trust was undermined by self-orientation made evident in an age when social media enabled all to be seen and questioned.

We now live in an interstitial period where social media has accelerated a loss of trust. "Fake" is now more powerful than "authentic" in terms of expectations from commercial and political communications. There are many insights that could make up an analysis of the decline of trust after the Mass-Age. However, the Studioriley team settled on three related conversations, each of which helped us imagine a way forward on the journey to reestablishing trust in both media and the institutions that relate to their public through media.

The first was the simple observation that, after the Mass-Age, we have entered a period where a lack of agreed ethics (or the constraints of governmental regulation) have undermined our ability to recreate trust and enable the broad narratives that anchor society and culture. The second was that culture itself was transforming from a global hierarchy dominated by the West—suppressing both ancient and local cultures with the irresistible force of mass media, scientific argument, and patriarchal prejudice—to a network of many diverse local cultures, empowered by social media and elevated by global economics. As cultural power is unleashed, the social sciences provide an inadequate tool for understanding unless complemented by the kind of insight that comes from a creative perspective and learning process. Science can explain some aspect of society, but culture is what coheres society with shared meaning and the complexity of multiple narratives. In consequence, a third observation was that leadership is both essential and lacking in this new cultural context. The command-and-control generals of the mass market, the Jack Welch types of the world, are ineffective in a social media world where the generals cannot command and control the media through status or financial power. These old power structures are being replaced by creative leadership of collaborations. Listening is personal, because everyone is intimately connected. During the Mass-Age, intimacy was as scarce as hen's teeth, but it is now returning as a powerful mode of interpersonal communication. Old brands, representing old institutional values that were molded in the age of mass media, are failing as new competitors—vying for ideas, and for the hearts and minds—offer an intimate and congruent experience. The erosion of leadership is slowing down and will be reversed by cooperative, listening-focused organizations led by people who understand how to create the collaborations needed to innovate.

Leadership itself is being challenged to become a service, not an authority—a service that elevates the power of the individual within a collaborative framework fueled by creative exchange and insight. Such leaders already thrive within creative communities and creative enterprises. But toward the end of the Mass-Age, their value was diminished by rationalists who thought technology was not a tool but an answer. Big Data may provide big pictures using complex algorithms and big numbers, but none of this is worthwhile without meaning. Scientific knowledge alone has no ethical boundaries, because it is amoral. Science is experimentation, replication, and theory, but it is not a tool for organizing society; that job falls to culture. It is the creative among us—the poets, architects, choristers, DJs, storytellers, art directors— who will share their insights, feed our intuition, and enable inspiration. After the Mass-Age, the core competencies of a modern leader are the abilities to lead the cultural conversation, to abandon those conversations that are simply not needed, and to sit confidently with the unknown. Leadership in service of creative collaboration was Apple under Steve Jobs, and will be a template for future ways of innovating.

Congruence is the new goal. All can be seen in the social media age, so all needs to be aligned. Trust is about clarity, not dissonance, so congruence—throughout the organization, across all media, and on the ground in the experience of the product or service—has become the entry point for the creation of trust. *The power of creative collaboration* is in the deployment of generative leadership, an environment in which the people being led feel they are doing their best work, and the broad audience experiences congruence across all media. And finally, all is made more effective when we deploy those collaborative leaders in search of the simple truths that can provide the foundation upon which congruence is built.

The illusions of the Mass-Age—brands representing untruths, politicians playing with concepts to obscure and "spin" reality—are being challenged by a public that sees congruence, authenticity, and clarity. When it comes to trust, obfuscation destroys it, self-interest undermines it, and incongruence erodes it. Perhaps as important is the fact that the Mass-Age eradicated history in favor of fashion, of the "now" rather than the "then." The past became mere history rather than a path to the present and future. But as we see people all over the world embrace social media to investigate who they are along with what they can learn and do, we see the past coming back into focus, defining cultural expression and offering continuity, stability, and identity in very confusing times. Trust is now a product of a clear understanding of the cultures, as well as the desires and needs, of those being served. The trusted know the trusting.

Leadership creates trust after the Mass-Age by serving collaborations. It is too tempting to try out a "powerful" leader, one who "takes no prisoners" and is "in command of the situation." These concepts are tiresome. They are part of an old man's monologue and are doomed in this world of multiple competing narratives, of diversity glued by global economics. As Oxford Martin Fellow Chris Kutarna has claimed, "The basic problem is that 21st-century humanity is *tangled* together now—and not, as people say, 'connected.'" After the Mass-Age, it is clear we do not know all and can only begin to learn by opening ourselves to learning from others, in community, through collaboration.

Leaders can create fear and they can create trust. The latter is leadership as service. This means being driven by communal aspirations, desires, and needs. It means putting aside self-interest and offering integrity in an open and collaborative context. It is a leadership mode that accelerates learning, innovation, and perhaps more powerfully, our journey to peace. ▲

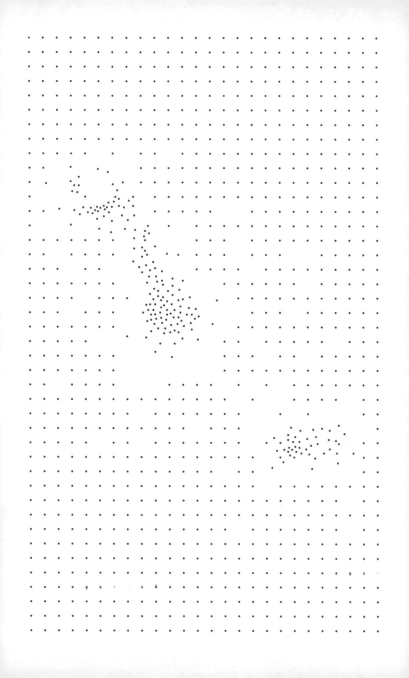

coda

This book is the beginning of a conversation, not an end. There are so many subjects to explore, conversations to be had, differences to be discussed. We will continue the conversation. We will add insights and challenging perspectives. We will seek the views of people from all contexts and places. We will immerse ourselves in the multiple and maybe competing narratives of life after the Mass-Age.

Over the years I have learned that time works on many levels. Sometimes the stories of the day are nothing more than passing trends and fast fashions, and the memes are interesting but inconsequential. But sometimes they reflect deeper, slower, powerful change. Such is true for gender issues, which are redefining societies and re-energizing cultures all over the world. Sometimes it is these slower changes—moving along in geologic time, it seems, through conversations that occur across lifetimes and between generations—that are the most profound and affect us most dramatically.

When I was at college in the 1970s, I participated in two conversations in the Geography department that have increased in relevance today, some forty years later. The first was "Trade or Aid with the Third World." This conversation is now a defining element of our modern world. People like myself, and many of the clients at Studioriley, have abandoned the old imperial idea of "Third World" in favor of "Majority World," and today we see those regions of humanity as offering culture, leadership, innovation, and economic growth. It is a different world, yet the same ignorance and prejudice continue to manifest in the way Western organizations think and operate.

The second conversation was about the impact of fossil fuels on the climate. I hardly need to say anything about this issue. After the Mass-Age, we are starting to deal with the consequences of an extract-and-exploit attitude to the world's resources; we have ignored the knowledge in spiritual traditions across our world of diverse cultures. Mass-Age thinking implies mass solutions. It is my view that when collaboration amongst diverse peoples in many different contexts is recognized as the way forward, we will increase our capacity to solve these massive environmental problems.

So the conversation continues. It should continue. Not as a conversation between elites in the ivory towers and sacred institutions, or even in the corporate headquarters and seats of government, but amongst us all—real people in real places.

In our work at Studioriley, we often study the research data provided by the World Values Survey, led by Professors Inglehart and Welzel. From their survey, which was conducted in nearly 100 countries and represents almost 400,000 interviews, it is one data point that always stands out: We all want to create a world that enables our children to live better lives than we do.

It is the power of our species to adapt and to evolve. The future conversations will be collaborative. We will throw off the shadow of the colonial era and go beyond the "dictatorship of reason" to listen more deeply and carefully to each other and the world around us. Those of us in global business have an amazing invitation: to help lead these conversations and manifest the collaborations needed to solve problems large and small. ▲

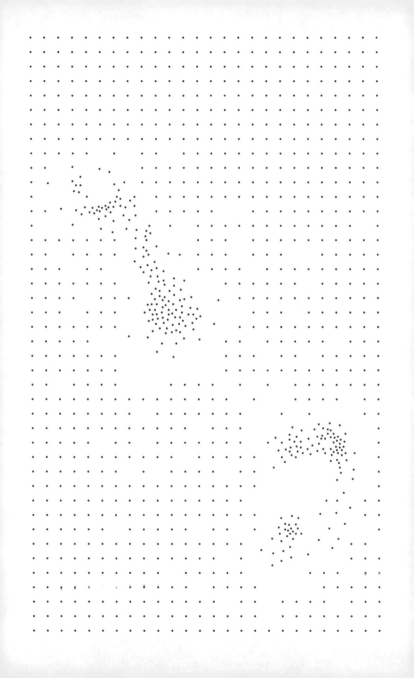

photographers

Akintunde Akinleye

Lagos, Nigeria
www.akintundeakinleye.com

Shahidul Alam

Dhaka, Bangladesh
www.drik.net

Vinicius Assencio

São Paulo, Brazil
www.cargocollective.com/viniciusassencio

Miss Bean

Hong Kong, China
www.missbeanbean.net

Jessica Cross

New York, NY and San Francisco, CA, U.S.A.
Cape Town, South Africa
www.crossxcolours.com

Andre Cypriano

Rio de Janeiro, Brazil
www.andrecypriano.com

Melanie Dunea

New York, NY, U.S.A.
www.melaniedunea.com
@melaniedunea

Noriko Hayashi

Tokyo, Japan
www.norikohayashi.com

photographers

Tony Karumba

Nairobi, Kenya
Twitter @tkarumba

Julie Keefe

Portland, OR, U.S.A.
www.juliekeefe.org

Zishaan Akbar Latif

Mumbai and New Delhi, India
www.zishaanakbarlatif.com

Wang Lei

Beijing, China

Moeketsi Moticoe

Johannesburg, South Africa
www.instagram.com/moeketsi_moticoe

Ben Nelms

Vancouver, BC, Canada
www.bennelms.ca

Edy Purnomo

Jakarta, Indonesia
www.instagram.com/edypur_pix/

Raghu Rai

New Delhi, India
www.magnumphotos.com/photographer/raghu rai

Marcela Taboada

Oaxaca, Mexico
www.marcelataboada.com

Newsha Tavakolian

Tehran, Iran
www.newshatavakolian.com

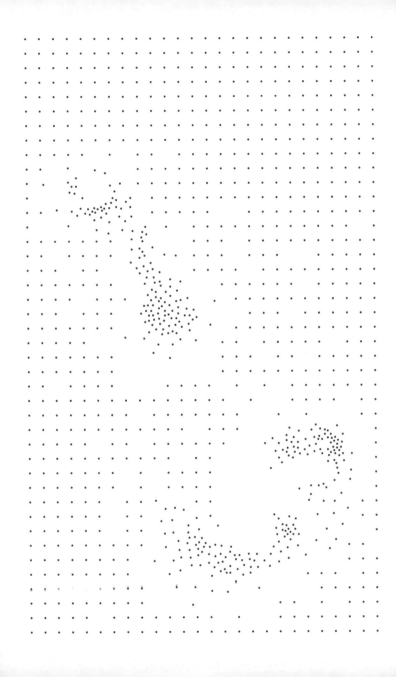

bibliography

preface

Saul, John Ralston. *Voltaire's Bastards: The Dictatorship of Reason in the West*. New York: The Free Press, 1992.

introduction

Alam, Shahidul. "Majority World: Challenging the West's Rhetoric of Democracy." *Amerasia Journal* 34, no. 1. (2008): 87–98.

Andersson, Benny and Björn Ulvaeus. "Money, Money, Money," from *Arrival*. Performed by ABBA. New York: Atlantic Records, 1976. Vinyl.

Armstrong, Neil. "One Giant Leap for Mankind." Transcript of remarks, Apollo 11 moon landing, July 20, 1969. NASA.

Benn, Tony. "Sonic Booms and I Hat E on the End. Tony Benn Remembers His Role in Getting Concorde Off the Ground." *The Guardian*. October 17, 2003.

Brand, Stewart, ed. *Whole Earth Catalog*, no. 1010. Fall 1968. Menlo Park, CA: Portola Institute, 1968.

Churchill, Winston. "Winston Churchill: Great Speeches of the 20th Century: 'We Shall Fight on the Beaches.'" Delivered June 4, 1940 at the House of Commons, United Kingdom. *The Guardian*. April 20, 2007.

Cline, Seth. "The Other Symbol of George W. Bush's Legacy." *U.S. News & World Report*. May 1, 2013.

Dobbs, Richard, and James Manyika, et al. *No Ordinary Disruption: The Four Global Forces Breaking All the Trends*. New York: PublicAffairs. 2015.

Dylan, Bob. "The Times They Are a-Changin'" from *The Times They Are a-Changin'*. Performed by Bob Dylan. New York: Columbia, 1964. Vinyl.

Edwards, Gavin. "'We Are the World': A Minute-by-Minute Breakdown on Its 30th Anniversary." *Rolling Stone*. March 6, 2015.

Eno, Brian. "Andrew Carnegie Lectures Series–Brian Eno." May 10, 2016. YouTube video, 1:35:32, posted by University of Edinburgh, January 19, 2017.

Estrin, James. "Wresting the Narrative from the West." *The New York Times*. July 19, 2013.

Forde, Steven. "John Locke and the Natural Law and Natural Rights Tradition." Natural Law, Natural Rights, and American Constitutionalism, nlnrac.org. Princeton, NJ: Witherspoon Institute, 2011.

Frum, David. "The Souring of American Exceptionalism." *The Atlantic*. July 3, 2017.

Gamble, Kenneth, Leon Huff, and Anthony Jackson. "For the Love of Money," from *Ship Ahoy*. Performed by The O'Jays. Philadelphia: Philadelphia International Records, 1973. Vinyl.

Gordy, Berry and Janie Bradford. "Money (That's What I Want)," from *With the Beatles*. Performed by The Beatles. Germany: Parlophone, 1963. Vinyl.

Guier, Spencer. "John Locke's Influence on the United States Constitution." Guier Law. 2017.

Horgan, John. "Is 'Social Science' an Oxymoron? Will That Ever Change?" *Scientific American*. April 4, 2013.

Independence Hall Association. "2. Foundations of American Government." American Government. USHistory.org.

"Is There Such a Thing as Social Science?" *Scientific American* 21, no. 20: 313. November 13, 1869.

Kennedy, Robert F. "Robert F. Kennedy Speeches: Remarks at the University of Kansas, March 18, 1968." JFKlibrary.org.

Knopfler, Mark and Sting. "Money for Nothing," from *Brothers in Arms*. Performed by Dire Straits. United Kingdom/Burbank, CA: Vertigo/Warner Bros. Records, 1985. Vinyl.

Kraynak, Robert P. "Thomas Hobbes: From Classical Natural Law to Modern Natural Rights." Natural Law, Natural Rights, and American Constitutionalism, nlnrac.org. Princeton, NJ: Witherspoon Institute, 2011.

Lehrer, Jonah. *Imagine: How Creativity Works*. Boston: Houghton Mifflin Harcourt, 2012.

Lennon, John and Paul McCartney. "All You Need Is Love," from *Magical Mystery Tour* and the *Our World* telecast. Performed by The Beatles. Germany/Los Angeles: Parlophone/Capitol Records, 1967. Vinyl.

Locke, John. *Second Treatise of Government*. C.B. Macpherson, ed. Indianapolis, IN: Hackett Publishing Company, 1980.

McLuhan, Marshall. *Understanding Media: The Extensions of Man*. New York: Signet Books, 1964.

McLuhan, Marshall. *The Medium Is the Massage: An Inventory of Effects*. New York: Random House, 1967.

McLuhan, Marshall, with John Lennon and Yoko Ono. "John Lennon & Yoko Ono Interview with Marshall McLuhan Part 1." December 20, 1969. YouTube video, 18:43, posted by Shavon Slyvia, September 25, 2016.

Nielsen Ratings. "Nielsen Celebrates 90 Years of Innovation." Nielsen.com. August 23, 2013.

Our World. International satellite television broadcast featuring The Beatles, Maria Callas, Pablo Picasso, et al. Produced by Aubrey Singer. BBC: June 25, 1967.

Press Association. "Brian Eno Calls for Rethink About Meaning and Value of Culture." *The Guardian*. September 27, 2015.

Rozell, Mark J. and Jeremy D. Mayer, eds. *Media Power, Media Politics*. Lanham, MD: Rowman and Littlefield Publishers, 2008.

Stratford, Sarah-Jane. "Referring to JFK's Presidency as 'Camelot' Doesn't Do Him Justice." *The Guardian*. November 21, 2013.

Toffler, Alvin. *The Third Wave*. New York: Morrow, 1980.

Trow, George W.S. "Within the Context of No-Context." *The New Yorker*. November 17, 1980.

Walt, Stephen M. "The Myth of American Exceptionalism." *Foreign Policy*. October 11, 2011.

Waters, Roger. "Money," from *The Dark Side of the Moon*. Performed by Pink Floyd. United Kingdom: Harvest, 1973. Vinyl.

1: the decline of trust after the mass-age

Cavendish, Richard. "The Soviet Union Is First to the Moon." *History Today* 59, no. 9. September 2009.

Chen, Lulu Yilun and David Ramli. "The Great Firewall of China." Bloomberg News. October 12, 2017; updated November 30, 2017.

Dobbs, Richard, James Manyika, and Jonathan Woetzel. *No Ordinary Disruption: The Four Global Forces Breaking All the Trends*. New York: PublicAffairs, 2015.

Edelman Intelligence. "2017 Edelman Trust Barometer, Global Report." *Edelman Trust Barometer 2017 Annual Global Study*. Chicago: Edelman, Inc., 2017.

Edelman Intelligence. "2017 Executive Summary." *Edelman Trust Barometer 2017 Annual Global Study*. Chicago: Edelman, Inc., 2017.

Green, Charles H., David H. Maister, and Robert M. Galford. *The Trusted Advisor*. New York: Free Press, 2000.

Kennedy, John F. "1962–09–12 Rice University." Transcript.
John F. Kennedy Presidential Library and Museum.

Kennedy, John F. "President John F. Kennedy at Rice University."
Excerpt. NASA Content Administrator, ed. Posted by NASA,
November 22, 2013; updated August 4, 2017.

Pew Research Center. "Public Trust in Government: 1958–2017."
Pew Research Center. May 3, 2017.

Pew Research Center. "Public Trust in Government Remains Near
Historic Lows as Partisan Attitudes Shift." Pew Research Center.
May 3, 2017.

Stirone, Shannon. "The Real Cost of NASA Missions: How Much
Are We Really Paying to Explore the Universe?" *Popular Science*.
November 4, 2015.

U.S. and World Population Clock. United States Census Bureau.
Census.gov.

Weiner, Tim. "Theodore C. Sorensen, 82, Kennedy Counselor, Dies."
The New York Times. October 31, 2010.

2: the power of ethics after the mass-age

Bigman, Alex. "Four Principles by Paul Rand That May Surprise You."
99designs.com. 2012.

Carlin, George. "Seven Words You Can Never Say on Television,"
from *Class Clown*. Performed by George Carlin. New York:
Little David/Atlantic Records, 1972. Vinyl.

Clinton, George, Walter Morrison, and Garry Shider. "One Nation
Under a Groove," from Funkadelic. Performed by *Funkadelic*.
Burbank, CA: Warner Bros. Records, 1978. Vinyl.

"Deconstructing Radical Transparency: An Interview with
Michael Preysman, Founder & CEO, Everlane." ProjectJUST.com.
March 8, 2017.

Gerstner, Lou. "Lou Gerstner on Corporate Reinvention and Values."
Interview with Ian Davis and Tim Dickson. *McKinsey Quarterly*.
September 2014.

Haidt, Jonathan. *The Righteous Mind: Why Good People Are Divided
by Politics and Religion*. New York: Pantheon Books, 2012.

Heller, Steven. *Paul Rand*. London: Phaidon Press, 1999.

McCormack, Nic. "What Goes Into Making an Earth-Friendly
$68 Pair of Jeans." *Bloomberg*. October 6, 2017.

Montagna, Maggie and Mortimer Singer. "Op-Ed: Why Mindful
Millennials Are Modern Pagans." *The Business of Fashion*.
November 7, 2017.

O'Toole, Mike. "At Everlane, Transparent Is the New Black."
    Forbes. January 5, 2016.

Quito, Anne. "How to Design an Enduring Logo: Lessons from
    IBM and Paul Rand." Quartz.com. July 23, 2015.

Rand, Paul. *Eye, Bee, M (IBM)*. 1981. Offset lithograph, 91.6 × 61.1 cm.
    Collection of Cooper Hewitt.

Rand, Paul. "The Politics of Design." In *Paul Rand: A Designer's Art*.
    New Haven, CT: Yale University Press, 1988.

Vanhemert, Kyle. "Paul Rand, The Visionary Who Shows Us That
    Design Matters." *Wired*. April 6, 2015.

Zarkin, Michael J. *The FCC and the Politics of Cable TV Regulation,
    1952–1980: Organizational Learning and Policy Development*.
    Amherst, NY: Cambria Press, 2010.

3: the re-emergence of culture after the mass-age

Andrews, Travis M. "From Kennedy to Trump, the Much-Deplored
    History of Presidential Candidates on Late-Night TV."
    The Washington Post. September 22, 2016.

Baker, Kevin. "Thanks, Trump! What He Got Right About
    American Democracy." *New Republic*. November 11, 2016.

Barrett, Paul and Matthew Philips. "Can ExxonMobil Be Found
    Liable for Misleading the Public on Climate Change?"
    Bloomberg Businessweek. September 7, 2016.

Bilefsky, Dan. "Alarmed Britons Ask Pollsters: Why Didn't You
    Warn Us?" *The New York Times*. June 24, 2016.

Boren, Cindy. "Nike's New 'Pro Hijab' Line Will Help Muslim
    Women Compete While Staying Covered." *Chicago Tribune*.
    March 7, 2017.

Brown, Paul. "Global Warming is Killing Us Too, Say Inuit."
    The Guardian. December 10, 2003.

Dunford, Daniel and Ashley Kirk. "How Right or Wrong Were the Polls
    About the EU Referendum?" *The Telegraph*. June 27, 2016.

Feynman, Richard. "The Brownian Movement." *The Feynman Lectures
    of Physics, Volume I* online from California Institute of Technology.
    Chapter 41-1: 1963.

Fischer, Douglas. "Climate Risks as Conclusive as Link Between
    Smoking and Lung Cancer." *Scientific American*. March 19, 2014.

Hilts, Philip J. "Tobacco Chiefs Say Cigarettes Aren't Addictive."
    The New York Times. April 15, 1994.

Horizon (BBC)/*Nova* (PBS). "The Pleasure of Finding Things Out," interview with Richard Feynman. Season 18, Episode 9. Directed by Christopher Sykes. BBC: November 23, 1981.

Jacoby, Jeff. "Obama a Unifying Force? Hardly." *The Boston Globe.* April 22, 2012.

Kaufman, Alexander C. "Nike is Now Making Most of Its Shoes From Its Own Garbage." *Huffington Post.* May 11, 2016.

Kell, John. "Nike Takes a Stand for Equality in Politically-Charged America." *Fortune.* February 13, 2017.

Lennon, John and Paul McCartney. "All You Need Is Love," from *Magical Mystery Tour.* Performed by The Beatles. Germany/ Los Angeles: Parlophone/Capitol Records, 1967. Vinyl.

Loria, Kevin and Reuters. "Harvard Researchers Have Found Evidence That Exxon Misled the Public on Climate Science." *Business Insider.* August 24, 2017.

Marley, Bob. "One Love," from *The Wailing Wailers.* Performed by The Wailers. Kingston, Jamaica: Studio One, 1965. Vinyl.

Mercer, Andrew, Claudia Deane and Kyley McGeeney. "Why 2016 Election Polls Missed Their Mark." Pew Research Center. November 9, 2016.

Nike. "Top Things to Know About Sustainable Innovation at Nike." Nike News online. May 11, 2016.

Rao, Vidya. "President Obama Can Let Loose on Late-Night TV, Thanks to Bill Clinton." Today.com. August 7, 2013.

Sable, David. "Bypassing Media and Speaking Straight to the People: Crime or Evolution?" *Huffington Post.* January 23, 2017.

Segran, Elizabeth. "Meet the Muslim Woman Who Inspired Nike to Enter the Hijab Business." *Fast Company.* April 24, 2017.

Walsh, Bryan. "How Climate Change is Disrupting the Inuit of Clyde River." Time.com. July 12, 2017.

4: the nature of leadership after the mass-age

Bariso, Justin. "Uber's New CEO Just Sent an Amazing E-mail to Employees—and Taught a Major Lesson in Emotional Intelligence." Inc.com. September 23, 2017.

Bass, Dina. "Ballmer by the Numbers: How Microsoft Has Fared During the CEO's Reign." *Bloomberg.* October 24, 2013.

Beer, Jeff. "Apple, Google, and Microsoft Ranked Three Most Valuable Global Brands of 2017," *Fast Company* September 26, 2017.

Chase, Jefferson. "AfD: What You Need to Know About Germany's Far-Right Party." DW.com. September 24, 2017.

Dejevsky, Mary. "This Is What Emmanuel Macron's First Cabinet Tells Us About How the French President Will Govern." *The Independent*. May 18, 2017.

Demmitt, Jacob. "New Era: Microsoft CEO Satya Nadella Speaks at Salesforce Conference, Gives iPhone Demo." Geekwire.com. September 16, 2015.

Eichenwald, Kurt. "Microsoft's Lost Decade." *Vanity Fair*. July 24, 2012.

Ferguson, Niall. "Networks and Hierarchies." *The American Interest* 9, no. 6. June 9, 2014.

Fiegerman, Seth. "Uber's New CEO: 'This Company Has to Change.'" CNN Tech. August 30, 2017.

Groysberg, Boris and Michael Slind. "Leadership Is a Conversation." *Harvard Business Review*. June 2012.

Hempel, Jessi. "Restart: Microsoft In the Age of Satya Nadella." *Wired*. February 2015.

Della Cava, Marco. "Microsoft's Satya Nadella Is Counting on Culture to Drive Growth." *USA Today*. February 20, 2017.

Henley, Jon. "German Elections 2017: Angela Merkel Wins Fourth Term But AfD Makes Gains–As It Happened." *The Guardian*. September 24, 2017.

Ikenberry, G. John. *"Soft Power: The Means to Success in World Politics* by Joseph S. Nye, Jr." Review. *Foreign Affairs*. May/June 2004.

Jobs, Steve. "Steve Jobs iPhone 2007 Presentation." YouTube video, 51:18, posted by Jonathan Turetta, May 13, 2013.

Kotter, John P. "Hierarchy and Network: Two Structures, One Organization." *Harvard Business Review*. May 23, 2011.

Kuek Ser, Kuang Keng. "Trump Is Ending Obama-Era Emissions Cuts. How Will CO^2 Emissions Change?" PRI/Public Radio International. March 28, 2017.

Libby, Brian. "The Connector: Talking with Donald Stastny, AFO's 2017 Honored Citizen." Portland Architecture: A Blog About Design in the Rose City. October 2017.

McAuley, James. "Emmanuel Macron: A United Europe Is the Best Weapon Against the Far Right." *The Washington Post*. September 26, 2017.

Metz, Cade. "Tech Time Warp of the Week: Watch Steve Ballmer Laugh at the Original iPhone." *Wired*. September 5, 2014.

Nonaka, Ikujiro and Hirotaka Takeuchi. "The Big Idea: The Wise Leader." *Harvard Business Review*. May 2011.

NPR. "Former Rep. Bob Inglis on Trump Environmental Regulation Rollbacks." *Morning Edition.* NPR. March 29, 2017.

NPR. "How Do You Turn Around a Tech Giant? With Empathy, Microsoft CEO Says." *All Things Considered.* NPR. September 25, 2017.

Ranger, Steve. "Goodbye Windows Phone: What Comes Next for Microsoft in Mobile?" ZDnet.com. July 13, 2017.

Rothfeder, Jeffrey. "For Honda, Waigaya Is the Way." *Strategy+Business* 76, Autumn 2014. August 1, 2014.

Samuel, Henry. "How Does the French Political System Work and What Are the Main Parties?" *The Telegraph.* May 7, 2017.

Schoemaker, Paul J.H. and Steven Krupp. "Six Principles That Made Nelson Mandela a Renowned Leader." *Fortune.* December 5, 2014.

Sherman, Eric. "Microsoft to Lay Off 18,000." CBSnews.com. July 17, 2014.

5: the role of creative collaboration after the mass-age

Browne, David. "'The Defiant Ones': Dr. Dre and Jimmy Iovine's Wild Adventure." *Rolling Stone.* July 7, 2017.

Buck, Sebastian. "As Millennials Demand More Meaning, Older Brands Are Not Aging Well." *Fast Company.* October 5, 2017.

"Chrysler Eminem Super Bowl Commercial – Imported from Detroit." YouTube video, 2:03, posted by Chrysler, February 5, 2011.

Cunningham, Lillian. "Myers-Briggs: Does It Pay to Know Your Type?" *The Washington Post.* December 14, 2012.

Cusumano, Michael A. "Manufacturing Innovation: Lessons from the Japanese Auto Industry." *MITSloan Management Review.* Fall 1988.

Elmer-DeWitt, Philip. "Mac vs. PC: Inside the Ad Wars." *Fortune.* August 30, 2009.

Farber, Jim. "Donny McCaslin on David Bowie: 'We Had This Amazing Connection, Then He Was Gone.'" *The Guardian.* October 4, 2016.

Gianatasio, David. "Nike's 'Just Do It,' the Last Great Advertising Slogan, Turns 25: W+K Celebrates a Milestone." *Adweek.* July 2, 2013.

Greene, Andy. "The Inside Story of David Bowie's Stunning New Album, 'Blackstar.'" *Rolling Stone.* November 23, 2015.

Halban, Tania. "Philip Glass Turns 75: 'Koyaanisqatsi', Ravi Shankar Collaboration 'Passages,' and 'Satyagraha.'" Notesonnotes.org. December 15, 2012.

Hayden, Steve. "'1984': As Good as It Gets." *Adweek*.
    January 30, 2011.

Humphrey, Nicholas. *The Inner Eye: Social Intelligence in Evolution*.
    Oxford, U.K.: Oxford University Press, 2003.

Komlik, Oleg. "Albert Einstein on the Power of Ideas and Imagination
    in Science." Economicsociology.org. January 8, 2016.

Kutarna, Chris. "Does Democracy Still Work?" Kutarna.net.
    October 8, 2017.

"Lee Clow: Apple's 'Think Different' Ad Guru Steps Down from
    Post as Chief Creative Officer (VIDEO)." HuffingtonPost.com.
    March 18, 2010.

Maslow, Abraham H. "A Theory of Human Motivation." *Psychological
    Review* 50, no. 4. (1943): 370–396.

Microsoft News. "Satya Nadella Email to Employees on First
    Day as CEO." Microsoft News Center. February 4, 2014.

Murray, Martin. "Manufacturing Process." The Balance.
    February 3, 2017.

Pareles, Jon. "Ascending Without Zeppelin: Robert Plant Releases
    'lullaby and The Ceaseless Roar.'" *The New York Times*.
    September 7, 2014.

Rawlinson, Nik. "History of Apple: The Story of Steve Jobs and the
    Company He Founded." MacWorld UK. April 25, 2017.

Roberts, Sam. "Bill Backer, Who Taught the World (and Don Draper)
    to Sing, Dies at 89." *The New York Times*. May 16, 2016.

Roman, Ken. "A Look Back at Hal Riney, the Contrarian: Ad Giant
    Helped Re-Elect Ronald Reagan." *Ad Age*. March 23, 2016.

Siegel, Alan. "'Bud-Weis-Er': The Origin Story of the
    Super Bowl-Famous Budweiser Frogs." *USA Today* Ad Meter.
    January 13, 2015.

Stancati, Margherita. "When Ravi Shankar Met George Harrison."
    The Wall Street Journal. December 12, 2012.

Statista.com. "TV Viewership of the Super Bowl in the United States
    from 1990 to 2017 (in Millions)." Statista.com. February 2017.

Welzel, Christian. *Freedom Rising: Human Empowerment and the
    Quest for Emancipation*. Cambridge, U.K.: Cambridge
    University Press, 2013.

Yarow, Jay. "Apple Ad God Lee Clow's Work – A Look Back."
    Business Insider. October 30, 2009.

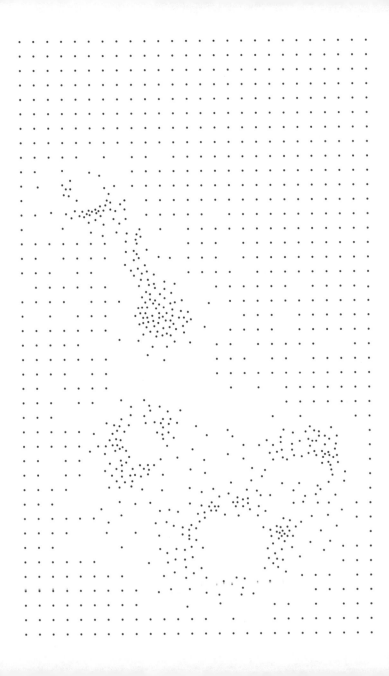

acknowledgments

This book is a collaborative effort and would not have been created were it not for all the people credited in our colophon. I may be the author, but it was often the wise words and thoughtful commentary of each member of the team that turned it from the ravings of a mad man to something loosely resembling sanity. I acknowledge and thank you all. Each and every photographer provided a wealth of insight, a wonder of context, and permission to use their work in this book. I give thanks and delighted acknowledgments to them for that. I would also like to acknowledge the inspiration and mentoring I have received from Dan Wieden and David Kennedy, who employed me way back in the Mass-Age and encouraged me to think wildly and be edited thoroughly.

Finally, thank you, a thousand times thank you, to Chris Rainier and Alex Chadwick for influencing the ideas presented here and encouraging them to emerge into the light.

colophon

Author
Chris Riley

Concept and Design
Fredrik Averin

Producer
Jade Wieting

Editor
Amanda Schurr

Copy Editor
Sheila Ashdown

Proof Reader
Matt Keppel

An An^log publication

First Edition

ISBN 978-0-9996425-0-4

about the author

Chris Riley leads Studioriley, which was founded in 2010 as a collaborative strategic insights and planning practice focused on global work, technology, and multicultural insights. From 2005 to 2010, he was head of strategic planning in Apple's MARCOM and graphic design group. From 2002 to 2005, he created and ran Studioriley V1.0, whose lead client was Nokia. From 1991 to 2002, he was head of strategic planning at advertising innovators Wieden+Kennedy, whose clients included Nike, Microsoft, and Coca-Cola. In all roles, he has been engaged in new markets, new geographies, and new practices. He has worked all over the world, considers himself a geographer at heart, and has been fortunate enough to collaborate with some of the finest creative minds imaginable.